How to Build Your Brand

How to Build Your Brand

Implementing a Proven and Effective Process

Laurence Lubin

Routledge
Taylor & Francis Group

A PRODUCTIVITY PRESS BOOK

First published 2022
by Routledge
605 Third Avenue, New York, NY 10158

and by Routledge
2 Park Square, Milton Park, Abingdon, Oxon, OX14 4RN

Routledge is an imprint of the Taylor & Francis Group, an informa business

ISBN: 9781032121499 (hbk)
ISBN: 9781032121468 (pbk)
ISBN: 9781003223313 (ebk)

DOI: 10.4324/9781003223313

Typeset in Garamond
by Deanta Global Publishing Services, Chennai, India

For my three sons, Robert, Michael, and Todd

Contents

PART III PROCESS VALIDATION

PART IV CASE HISTORIES

PART V EXECUTIVE INTERVIEWS

Acknowledgments

My sons inspired me to write the book. They envisioned a couple of tacks the book could take. One approach would capture amusing *Mad Men* stories from my early years in advertising. A book title under consideration at the time: *Branding Secrets of a Mad Man*. The other approach would join the battle of traditional marketing vs digital marketing…branding values of the FMCG school vs the "product" focus of the digital school.

The book I have written tells a different story. It's designed for marketing professionals who already know the basic philosophy and techniques of marketing. The book seeks to fill their desire to understand the creative process…solving open-ended, complex branding challenges.

My thanks must go to my colleagues at Grey and P&G – too many to mention. We had many big wins which, when I analyzed them years later, became the source of my Success Model.

Andrea Dunham and I worked together to understand and ultimately structure the creative process. She and I went on a three-year journey. There were no Professors of Creativity to consult. Without Andrea's intellectual curiosity, my Method would not have happened.

My partner and Lubin Lawrence co-founder, Barbara Lawrence, and I applied the Model for our clients over 30 years. The case histories from our practise are the backbone of the book. Without Barbara, there is no book.

My clients, many of whom are interviewed in this book, are the reason the Brand Platforms came to fruition. My clients' branding philosophy and leadership skills are the reason good things happened.

My consultants who did the analysis, developed the creative ideas, and conducted the research, helped prove the Method was effective. They also demonstrated the Method was teachable and repeatable.

My clients and my consultants were critical success factors. Their contributions were invaluable.

About the Author

Thirty years ago, Larry Lubin co-founded Lubin Lawrence with the mission to help companies invent or reinvent their brands. Larry started his career at Grey Advertising, working on the Procter & Gamble account. At the time he joined Grey, the agency had completed a multi-year, multi-brand study that proved that changes in attitudes predict changes in behavior. His P&G team applied the learning to develop a brand strategy to reinvent Jif Peanut Butter and invent Downy Fabric Softener.

The strategies changed consumers' attitudes, positively impacting their esteem: Jif moms for making good decisions for their kids' wellbeing (Choosy Moms Choose Jif) and kids appreciating Downy moms for all they do for them. Both brands became dominant market leaders and are enjoying decades of growth.

Larry developed the Model that explains why a few brands like Jif and Downy enjoy exceptional, long-term success. In essence, these brands are linked to the fundamental human values of the consumers they serve. The brands become more valuable because they honor the values consumers live by. With the Model in place, Larry went on a three-year journey to create the method to apply the model for corporate clients. The journey involved: (1) understanding the structure of the creative process, (2) developing visual research techniques to uncover tacit knowledge, and (3) researching academic literature to explain the model's success (*Descartes Error* by Damasio, *Homo Prospectus* by Seligman, *The Hero Within* by Pearson, *Hero of a Thousand Faces* by Campbell).

Larry's process has been applied for global clients who seek to gain a unique competitive advantage for their brands to include Disney, Procter & Gamble, PepsiCo, Heineken, and Colgate Palmolive. The Lubin Lawrence track record is based on branding building success with these and other clients. Larry's role at Lubin Lawrence is to lead client engagements, and help client teams and senior management engage with the process and commit to the brand solution.

Larry began teaching MBA students at NYU's School for Professional Studies. The course opened his mind to the idea of teaching professionals to learn the process: i.e., to solve complex, open-ended creative challenges Larry has created courses to teach the process to executives. Anyone interested in learning more about courses on creativity should email Larry at llubin@lubinlawrence.com.

Larry and his wife Sue have three sons, seven grandsons, and one granddaughter, Clementine. He and his wife enjoy spending time in any town named Chatham, presently Chatham, NJ and Chatham, MA. Larry graduated with honors from Harvard College.

Introduction: Why Did I Write the Book?

What is the book about and why did I write it? The book is about teaching my proven and effective brand building process. The input for the book is my branding experience over the past 30 years.

The book is written for marketing professionals who know what great branding looks like but do not have a step by step approach to achieving excellent branding results. As a consequence, brand development outcomes are frequently "hit or miss." Brand teams are in the "hit" business...similar to creating a hit song, or movie, or car. A client at a large, highly sophisticated marketing company described their branding process as "poke and hope."

To create the branding process, we spent years learning the structure of the creative process. There were no professors of creativity to consult. There were books that taught creative or generative techniques but no books on the first principles of creativity and how to apply them.

SETTING THE STAGE 1

Chapter 1

What Are the Shared Beliefs of Brand Driven Companies?

Leading academics like David Aaker and highly admired companies like Procter & Gamble are the industry thought leaders. They have codified the beliefs most companies have internalized and live by to include:

- brands are strategic assets and, as such, should be managed by highly experienced executives
- functional brand benefits are important but can usually be copied by competition
- brands should deliver emotional benefits to better bond with the target audience
- brands should become good story tellers because stories engage the whole brain and, as such, are more memorable
- brands should have a purpose that defines how they change consumers' lives for the better
- brands should guide a company's overall vision and mission along with the innovations that will create the future.

Most companies believe that they do not have a proven and effective brand building process in place. As a result, they often hire highly experienced marketing professional...CMOs...to create breakthrough brand initiatives. As we have all observed, the CMO position is highly volatile.

DOI: 10.4324/9781003223313-2

I suspect that the volatility reflects a few factors:

- it's very difficult to succeed in the "hit" business by its very nature. Most new brand initiatives fail. I suspect that's why books are written about the winners. "Victory has a thousand fathers, defeat is an orphan."
- traditional corporate success measures (e.g. sales, ROI) don't include or account for brand equity. Stated another way, companies get what they measure. And brand equity and emotions are hard to measure. And to date, impossible to measure in a way that can be expressed in a corporate earnings report.
- companies often don't invest sufficient funds or time to support brand initiatives.
- the survival politics of large organizations often works against the CMO as a "miracle worker" or "hit maker." Lightning in a bottle is probably the unwritten hope when hiring a CMO.

A few organizations never or rarely go outside to fill a CMO position. They hire and promote only those who began their careers with the company. They are usually quite adept at identifying and promoting those executives with natural or well above average branding skills. This approach favors success but is limited by the lack of a well- grounded and researched branding process.

Chapter 2

What Will Help the Reader Have a Successful Experience with This Book?

There are a number of factors, taken in concert, that will drive success:

- the reader should select a brand that he or she wants the process applied to. It can be a brand he wishes to create; a brand that needs to be reinvented. If a team of readers go through the process together, they may want to select a brand of strategic importance to their company. Senior management may agree to judge the final outcome...to reinforce the effectiveness of the process and the team's solution. Bottom line...the process should be applied to real world challenges in which the reader is deeply involved...and not a theoretical exercise.
- the reader should create a base line of self-knowledge before learning before reading the book. Here are some pre-read questions.

How does the reader define branding? What are the reader's favorite brand(s) and why?

What is the reader's branding experience? Does the reader follow a particular branding method? What branding questions or issues does the reader wish to address?

What is the reader's desired outcome from the book besides learning the process? For example, does the reader wish to learn about the structure of the creative process? Research techniques to uncover tacit knowledge? Brand

DOI: 10.4324/9781003223313-3

hypotheses generation? Brand concept development? Brand strategy development? Implementation tactics?

The reader can compare their in-going assumptions at any point along the way and at the conclusion of the book.

■ the reader will recognize that the brand building process is, in its essence, the creative process. As such, the reader is actually learning how to approach and manage complex creative work.

■ of all the work undertaken in corporations i.e. engineering, craft, and routine work, nothing is more difficult than creative work. That's because creative work has the most unknowns and most variables. All the steps of the branding process are based on academic studies and practical experience about the best way to manage complex creative challenges.

■ a company's corporate culture is stronger than steel. Peter Drucker was correct when he stated that: "Culture eats strategy for breakfast." Involving and collaborating with cross-functional teams help ensure alignment, that a transfer of learning takes place, and there is commitment to implement the brand solution. Net, net, the process includes activities to ensure that corporate culture is reflected in the brand solution.

Chapter 3

Where Did the Success Model Come from?

I joined Grey Advertising after graduating college. Grey had just completed a multi brand/multi-year study to determine if changes in brand attitudes would predict changes in brand behavior. The conclusion: changes in attitude did indeed predict changes in behavior. Brands with increased positive attitudes grew; brands with increased negative attitudes declined. No change in attitudes, no change in behavior.

We applied the insights from the study to develop brand strategies for two Procter & Gamble brands. Jif peanut butter, number three in the market after Skippy and Peter Pan, had seen volume decline for 13 consecutive years. And Downy, a fabric softener that P&G wanted to launch. Downy would be the fifth fabric softener in the US market. The other four brands had failed to make the fabric market viable. Household penetration of fabric softeners was under 1% pre- Downy.

Jif was relaunched with the tagline "Choosy Moms Choose Jif" honoring moms for making good decisions on their kids' behalf. Jif became market leader in five years and has remained so for decades.

Downy was launched with a campaign property that showed a mom holding a bath towel, hugging her child and a reverse image showing the kid hugging mom...expressing appreciation to mom for all that she does for him. The fabric softener market had household penetration of 70% within three years of Downy's launch and Downy had a 90% share of the market.

Jif's relaunch and Downy's launch had one element in common...both elevated the self-esteem of target consumers. Elevating self-esteem, honoring

DOI: 10.4324/9781003223313-4

the way the target consumer feels about herself, has a positive impact on brand attitudes. Jif, a brand in long decline, was reinvented in consumers' eyes. Downy, a new brand, established a unique emotional bond with consumers.

Importantly, Downy was able to persuade a vast array of consumers to add a fabric softener to their laundry routine. And Downy made the laundry routine more complex and time consuming because consumers had to add Downy at the midpoint of the washing machine cycle.

There is a rule in marketing that one should launch products that do not require consumers to change their habits. Our habits reflect ways we get things done efficiently.

Asking us to change our habits is considered extremely difficult to do even assuming we have the time and money to educate consumers on the benefits the change could bring.

That the Downy story had the power to change consumers' habits...in this case, making their laundry process less convenient...is testimony to the power of an aspirational brand story.

These two brands were key to the development of the Success Model.

BRAND BUILDING PROCESS

Chapter 4

What Is the Success Model and Why Is It Valid?: The Success Model

Brands that have demonstrated growth over long periods of time, despite the tests of competition, have merged the motivating power of fundamental human beliefs with their offering.

Why do brands that have applied the Success Model enjoy long-term success?

- Fundamental Human Beliefs answer the four questions all humans must answer. Who am I? Whom do I belong to? What is my mission in life? How capable am I? The answer to these questions creates meaning in our lives. When brands link their story to these beliefs, they become more valuable because they honor the values we live by.

These beliefs are above culture, country, and category. They are above culture which is always shifting. They are not tied to any one country's beliefs. They are the above category which is functionally defined.

In many ways, these beliefs reflect how the human species has made it to the top of the food chain. We humans are always imagining a better future for ourselves, our families and friends, and, in many cases, our world. We seek to connect with others to share joys and sorrows and build better

DOI: 10.4324/9781003223313-6

futures. Our fundamental beliefs give our lives meaning and shape the way we live.

■ Brands that have embraced the Success Model continue to grow over generations. The reason: Fundamental Human Beliefs do not change over time. New consumers entering a market share the same beliefs as the consumers who have participated in the market for decades. As such, Success Model brands don't "age out." They are renewed as a new generation of consumers enter the market.

Chapter 5

What Is the Method that Brings the Success Model to Life?

The Method was developed over three years in which we needed to first learn and then apply the principles of the creative process. There are three stages of the Method:

- Foundation Stage where we develop brand building hypotheses.
- Conceptualization Stage where we develop the brand concepts that express the brand hypotheses in consumer-facing language and imagery.
- Implementation Stage where we put in place the executional roadmap to bring the Brand Concepts to life all consumer touch points.

DOI: 10.4324/9781003223313-7

Chapter 5

What Is the Method that Brings the Success Model to Life?

Chapter 6

Foundation Stage

Step 1

The reader selects a brand she wants to apply the process to. It may be a brand the reader wants to create. Or a brand that needs reinvention. Or an opportunity to expand a brand portfolio. What's key is that the process is experienced solving a real world challenge. The goal is to increase the odds that the learning about the process takes place...that knowledge is transferred. Adults learn by doing!

Another option is that the book is used by a team of readers working together to apply the process. If such is the case, a reader team should consider involving senior management to evaluate their brand proposition to demonstrate the value of the process to both the readers and their management.

Step 2

The reader decides the goals for the branding effort. For example:

- to regain global leadership
- to justify premium pricing in a commoditized market
- to become a mainstream market leader
- to dominate a market segment.

The goals will drive the process.

DOI: 10.4324/9781003223313-8

Step 3

The reader needs to create the Business Framework to focus development of the brand building hypotheses. The wider and deeper the Framework, the greater the odds of creating a big branding idea. The Framework should contain all the factors the brand must satisfy to be successful, i.e. target audience definition, competitive landscape, distribution, profit drivers, company assets and capabilities, financial community, regulatory, supplier. All of these factors (plus any others the reader believes must be added) will focus brand hypothesis development. We view all factors as points on a star with the brand hypothesis and eventually the Brand Platform in the middle of the star.

Let's take the factors one by one:

- Target Audience Definition. The target should be the high potential prospects that are key to achieving your brand goals. In some cases, target definition is fairly obvious, e.g. when Amazon launched, their target was a consumer who buys books from bookstores. Over time, Amazon's target became consumers who shop at Walmart, Costco, and Kroger, and eventually everywhere.

In other cases, targeting is less clear, e.g. online universities initially viewed their target as "work first, life second" students who were on average in their early thirties, perhaps a parent with a full time job, seeking a degree to advance her career. Over time other targets seemed worth pursuing, e.g. students at community colleges who needed a flexible school schedule… lifetime learners of all ages including retirees seeking knowledge for knowledge's sake.

The important takeaway is that you should investigate all target segments that have the potential to help your brand reach its goals. You may have one, a few, or many legitimate target prospects. Each should be studied separately. In the end the most important prospects almost always become apparent. Your brand solution must win over these high value prospects. Even Amazon needed to decide, among all consumers buying books in a bookstore, which segments are most attractive. Consumers who love the experience of a bookstore are probably the least attractive segment. Consumers seeking a really convenient shopping experience are the best prospects and, as such, the prospects who should be the focus of website design.

In subsequent chapters we will discuss the research approach to generate the rich insight upon which brand hypotheses will be developed. At the outset of the process, we must identify the target segments we wish to study.

■ Competitive Landscape. If our company produces pet food for dogs and cats, our competition is other pet food companies. We may choose to compete against mainstream brands with mainstream pricing or high-end premium or super premium brands. If so, we need to learn about the corporate parents of our competition. Their scale, regional or country or global ambitions, their resources and willingness and ability to invest, their R&D capabilities etc. We need to learn if they have any vulnerabilities we can exploit, brand positionings we can trump.

We need to decide if our new brand can become a disrupter. Pampers disrupted the market(s) for cloth diapers. Disposable diapers did not exist pre-Pampers. Downy did not invent the fabric softener market but the brand created the story that made the market viable, and Downy, the dominant player. It's worth noting that P&G could no longer meet its corporate growth goals by growing share in its existing markets and needed to create new markets. Downy and Pampers are examples of using brands to create new markets.

Today, we are witnessing the disruption of traditional TV via Netflix and other streamers, retailing via Amazon, information via Google. Is our brand a disrupter?

The point is that we must think through how our new brand will compete. Can we play the same game competition plays, only better? Paper towels existed before Bounty. What Bounty did was reinvent the way paper was made (for the first time since the Egyptians) to establish brand leadership. The Bounty story of the "quicker picker upper" is as much about product innovation as brand storytelling. None-the-less, the business decision to enter the paper towel market preceded the creation of the brand strategy.

Can we play a new game like Pampers or Amazon?

■ Distribution. Where will we be distributed? Are we going direct to the consumer? Bricks and mortar retailers? E-commerce retailers? All the above? Is the trade our partner? Our competitor? Both? Can we insulate our brand with the right type of partnership? While we have an ultimate user or consumer target, we also may have a trade target. How should we manage the trade relationship?

■ Profit Drivers. How do we make money today? Are we low-cost produc-
ers? Toys R Us was able to price toys well below "mom and pop" retailers (whom they put out of business) until Walmart decided they wanted
a piece of the toy business. To do so, Walmart, with its ultra-flexible
distribution system, converted ten aisles to toys for the six weeks before
Christmas...selling toys at or below Toys R Us prices. Walmart was market leader within weeks and Toy R Us was finished.

Walmart made money by winning over consumers on the "big shopping"
occasion and not the smaller 3–4 times per week of traditional supermarkets. As a result, Walmart could sell toys at breakeven because the store traf-
fic they generated at Christmas more than paid for itself.

So again our question...what should be our distribution strategy?

■ Company Assets and Capabilities. Does our company have proprietary
skills or assets we can leverage? Do we invest more in R&D than our
competitors? Do we have a stronger sales force?

Are we willing to invest for the long term? If yes, are our competitors less
willing to do so?

What skills or technology do we have in hand that will give us an edge?

■ Financial Community. Assuming our company is a public enterprise,
what does the financial community think of us? Will they give us more
time to succeed with a new brand because they believe we are R&D
driven and have succeeded with new innovations even though we
could not meet quarterly EPS targets?
■ Regulatory. Are there government and non-government institutions
that will impact our brand proposition? How should we overcome any
potential barriers?
■ Supplier. Is our company vertically integrated? If so, how can we leverage that strength? If the company depends on suppliers, what is their
ability to impact brand performance? Can they impact pricing? Can they
disrupt the supply chain? Do they supply our competitors? Do they
impede innovation?

The Business Framework is designed to ensure we are considering the larger
factors that will impact our brand success. From a creative standpoint, the

Framework will inspire new ways for our brand to compete...creating the opportunity to insulate our brand from competition and reduce risk.

The Framework also helps with scenario building, i.e. exploring ways a market might evolve and competitors might react to our new brand proposition. The scenarios may not future proof a brand proposition, but they do force us to think through what might happen when direct or indirect competition reacts to our new brand.

Step 4

How does the reader populate the Business Framework?

Company proprietary studies. Studies and data in the public domain.

Executive and expert interviews within a company yield important insight. Our premise is that core beliefs that drive decisions are not in company studies. These beliefs are in the minds of the executives. That knowledge needs to be gathered to understand the barriers that need to be overcome...the cultural values to be addressed...to green light a new brand story.

When we conduct these interviews, we always ask four questions: Where is the company today? How did it get there? Where would you like to take the company in the future? What would hold you back from realizing your vision?

These four questions are deliberately designed to be open ended. They usually reveal the executive's big picture thinking that will impact the brand building process. When we conduct a number of interviews, we learn whether the company executives are aligned in their views or not. Either way we are learning about the issues we need to address internally to gain agreement to our brand proposition.

Another interview technique is to ask the executive to gather a few images that reflect his thinking on a key issue impacting the branding process. An alternative is to share

10–15 images with the executive and ask him to select the images that most reflect his thinking, e.g. images that link to the competitive landscape or his company's culture.

Imagery is a powerful language of strategy. Abstract concepts come alive when the executive selects a relevant image and tells us the story about why he selected that image and what it means to him.

Step 5

The previous four steps have gathered relevant knowledge and are structured in ways that the reader or a team of readers can access...net, net, the process now has a shared knowledge base. The reader must now use that knowledge to generate brand building hypotheses, i.e. benefits with the potential to create unique competitive advantage.

It's worth noting that idea generation is a divergent use of the mind, i.e. the perceptual and intuitive modes of thinking housed in the right brain. The left-brain houses logic. It is very powerful and usually overrules the right brain. One way to tap right brain perception is to not allow the left brain to take over. The reader can make that happen by recognizing that, when generating ideas, he must remain in the divergent mode, i.e. no left brain negativity allowed. When the reader feels he has generated a strong array of ideas, he can invoke the power of the left brain (convergent use of the mind) to make judgments. The key is to separate the divergent and convergent modes of thought.

A bit of history. During World War II, the US Government noted that Germany was more successful than the United States in developing patents for new technology. The government assembled German scientists living in the United States to understand why. The scientists explained that it was critical to their invention process to separate divergent from convergent thinking. If you converge too early, you kill good ideas and send negative signals to the people you are asking to generate those ideas. So keep generating ideas and even when you are sick of doing so, generate some more. Once you are done, you are ready to use your left-brain skills to judge your ideas.

Step 6

The reader needs to conduct qualitative research to develop brand hypotheses. The research is conducted among segments of the target market judged to be the best prospects for the brand opportunity.

The output from the research are Brand Platforms created by target segments. The Platforms are the brand hypotheses. Target consumers usually create 2–4 Brand Platforms in a research session.

There are several guiding principles that inform the creation of a Brand Platform:

- Each element of the Platform must be built separately. Complex creative problems need to be broken down into discrete components. Target consumers identify their Fundamental Human Beliefs; next they create their Desired Experience, then the brand's Unique Advantage, and last, the Unique Advantage Support.

The Beliefs and Desired Experience components are about the respondents' life. The Unique Advantage and Unique Advantage Support are about the Brand. When the respondents have separately developed the four elements of the Platform, they are asked to link the four elements of the Platform into a holistic story. Linkage is key. If the respondents can't link the elements, there is no story. The good news is that we have applied this research approach hundreds of times and we have not witnessed an instance when the respondents could not tell a holistic story.

I have outlined below the key elements of the research approach we use to develop Brand Platforms.

The research guide has several key exercises:

- Pre-Research Homework: The target will complete homework assignments to be discussed in the research. Example homework: gather 4–5 images that teach us who you are (Identity). Gather 4–5 images of your favorite brand (in the category the brand will compete in). Imagery uncovers tacit knowledge and makes it explicit so it can be addressed.
- Consumers are now asked to explain why they picked each top image. What did the image mean to them? How does it make them feel? Tell a story of what happened before the image and after the image. What can be done to make the image more ideal? Human thought is imaged based and two thirds of what we see is behind our eyes. As such, the images reveal deep truths about who we are and our hopes and dreams. Imagery gives us tacit knowledge that helps us determine the Fundamental Beliefs that anchor our Brand Platform. And the Desired experience of Brand Platform…what our imagination wishes will become our new reality.
- Research Mission: Consumers will be given their mission for the focus group which is to develop the ideal brand story that is unique and highly valuable to them. We find it useful to ask consumers to create the ideal brand story to give them the freedom to explore all

possibilities. If they are directed to create the Brand Platform for an existing brand in the market, they may be constrained by their existing feelings about the brand.

Once they create the ideal, they can be asked whether any brand on the market currently comes close to the ideal…or whether they believe a given brand could deliver the ideal. If yes, why yes. If no, why not.

- Consumers will be given the visual and verbal stimuli to build hypotheses, i.e. Brand Platforms that contain:
- Fundamental Human Beliefs statements, e.g. the connections between family and friends that give life meaning…living an authentic life …

Fundamental Human Belief Statements: Consumers are asked to select their favorite Belief statements. Examples of Belief statements: Close and Connected to the People who Give my Life meaning…Living Life to the Fullest. Their votes are tallied, and the moderator discusses the favorite Belief statements. The Beliefs are pinned to the wall. We have now identified one element of the Brand Platform… their favorite Beliefs statements.

- Consumers are now asked to link their favorite images to their favorite Belief statements. The selected images are highly aspirational. That is deliberate. We have learned that brands built on aspiration are very motivating. We have been asked if we should also explore images that respondents will hate. The assumption is that we can often gain good insight from why people dislike an image. Negative images can be instructive. For brand building, we focus on positive images because we are searching for consumer aspirations. We want to change consumers' lives for the better. We want to tap their imagination to glimpse their hopes and dreams.

Image Sort: Consumers are shown a battery of images and asked to say "yes" or "no," whether the image links to their beliefs and aspirations. For discussion's sake, let us assume the respondents are shown 50 images – maybe 25 are positive. The positive images are placed in a pile. The respondents are asked to sort the 25 images into discrete piles and to label each pile, e.g. family bonding, and to select the best family bonding image and place it on top of the pile.

The moderator discusses the best image of each pile. Why was it the best? What is the story behind the image? How can you make the image better? After the discussion, consumers are asked if any of the images link to any of the Belief statements. If so, why so. Consumers readily identify which images fit with which Beliefs and what the image adds to the Belief statement.

We now have two elements of the Brand Platform…Beliefs and Desired Experiences identified. Consumers usually develop 2–4 Brand Platform hypotheses.

Unique Advantage Statements. Consumers review and vote on the most important Unique Advantage or benefit statements. Benefits build businesses. The benefit statements are written to express a competitive advantage that consumers will really value. To create benefit statements, we need to think through the benefits delivered by the category or market within which we will compete. Can we deliver a meaningful advantage? Can we redefine the category bringing in new benefits, i.e. can our benefits "change the game" or "play the same game better"?

In some cases, we will create new benefits that are highly desirable, but respondents may find them not believable because they are too good to be true. We need to remind consumers that they are to keep their cognitive dissonance in check and assume that we can deliver the benefit. They should select the benefit if it's a favorite. Creating Unique Advantage may mean we need product innovation work in order to deliver important new benefits.

Pampers Stages Brand Platform is a good example. Consumers selected a benefit that Pampers support a baby's healthy growth and development. Consumers said that Pampers did not deliver that benefit nor did any other competitor. But if Pampers could deliver the benefit, that would be a game changer. P&G's R&D was initially stumped. The standing joke was "wear Pampers and go to Stanford!" Ultimately, R&D found the solution creating unique diapers for each stage of a baby's development e.g. Swaddlers and Cruisers.

The disposable diaper business is highly capital intensive. P&G believed the Stages Brand Platform more than met the expectations of target moms and, as such, made the investment to launch the new line. It's important to note that the benefits we create set expectations that our product or service must deliver against. Delivery must at a very minimum meet expectations.

Our goal is to develop concepts that exceed expectations. If delivery does not meet expectations, the Brand Platform should not be launched.

Clients tell us that they cannot deliver important new benefits and we should develop Unique Advantage statements that are feasible with their existing capabilities. My advice is to fight this suggestion. It may well be worth the innovation effort to deliver the new benefit. I have seen many brand companies deliver benefits that offer "imperceptible" product improvements. The usual result is wasted time and money behind an underwhelming brand benefit or story.

At this point we now have three elements of our Brand Platform once consumers have linked the Unique Advantage statements to the Beliefs and Desired Experience images.

Unique Advantage Support statements. These statements communicate how a Unique Advantage statement will be delivered. Pampers is a good example. Pampers Unique Advantage, "supporting baby's healthy growth and development" is delivered because Pampers has a diaper specifically designed to support each stage of the baby's development. The Stages product line brought the Unique Advantage to life for the target consumer... first-time moms.

The Platforms that emerge have all the elements above integrated into a holistic story.

The Brand Platform is a window into the consumer's mind. The power of the Platform is the connections respondents make between their Beliefs, Desired Experiences, a brand's Unique Advantage, and Unique Advantage Support.

The research produces Brand Platforms that contain the elements of the brand hypotheses expressed in a cohesive story. At the conclusion of the Foundation Stage, the reader has identified the best of the best Brand Platforms and why they are the most motivating.

Let's discuss the analysis we need to judge which Brand Platform or Platforms are the strongest hypotheses. In the case of Pampers, the Healthy Growth/Stages Platform was clearly head and shoulders above the rest. The first-time moms believed that benefit was a game changer, assuming Pampers could deliver it. The other benefits, e.g. softness against the baby's skin, were desirable but offered only an incremental improvement – not a game changer.

So in the case of Pampers, we had one Brand Platform that promised a Unique Advantage that was meaningful and superior to other Platforms.

In other cases, a few Brand Platforms may have strong appeal with target consumers. Our judgment supplemented by quantitative research may be needed to determine the strongest value proposition.

Other elements of the Business Framework can help build the case for the winning Platform. Pampers is again instructive. It would cost billions of dollars to upgrade Pampers factories to deliver the new Platform. It took a great deal of persuading to convince P&G's financial and manufacturing management to commit to an investment of that magnitude.

Competition would have a similar challenge should they choose to copy the new Pampers Platform. In the end, competition chose not to follow P&G. The result: Pampers created competitive insulation with capital investment as a barrier to entry.

The Pampers Platform justified premium pricing. Price leadership helped Pampers migrate from delivering the "me too" benefit of "keeping baby drier" to "different in kind" benefit that transformed the value of the category. The consumer research didn't prove Pampers could charge a premium, but target moms claimed they were willing to pay more.

The Pampers Platform suggested to consumers that the Brand was no longer only in the disposable diaper business. Pampers was in the "healthy growth" business which opened up other categories the Brand could enter, e.g. disposable wipes.

P&G's leadership role with the trade was enhanced. The trade doesn't win if one brand steals market share from another brand. They win if the category grows faster and becomes more profitable for them.

The key point of the above discussion is the need to make the case as to why the strongest Platforms can meet the goals we set at the outset of our brand building journey. At the end of the Foundation Stage, we need to make that case. Our Business Framework can help us think through the pluses and minuses of our Platform. In the end, we and senior management need to be convinced that the odds of winning are in our favor and, as such, we are enthusiastic about moving into the Conceptualization Stage.

Chapter 7

Conceptualization Stage

Step 7

The goal of this stage is to translate the Brand Platforms developed in the Foundation Stage into Brand Concepts. Brand Concepts will contain the words and images that clearly communicate the Platforms in a consumer facing form that is suitable for quantification. The elements of a Brand Concept are:

- a benefit statement that communicates the targets' aspiration and links to their Fundamental Human Beliefs
- an image that complements and/or supplements the benefit statement
- a benefit statement that communicates the Brand's Unique Advantage and Unique Advantage Support.

With the Brand Concepts in hand, the next step is to evaluate and refine the concepts in consumer research. The research is conducted among the best prospects for the new brand. The research plan, screener to recruit target prospects and guide for Conceptualization Research, will be outlined in a way to ensure the reader can implement it.

At the conclusion of the Conceptualization Stage, the reader will have the best of the best Brand Concepts along with the reasons the Concepts can fulfill the project goal.

The global flat chips (Lays) project offers an example of Brand Concept. Potato chip lovers of all ages and in all geographies believed potato chips are harmony. Potato chips are consumed on many occasions...at lunch with

DOI: 10.4324/9781003223313-9

a sandwich, alone reading a good book, when families and friends gather together to enjoy each other's company and, on occasion, celebrate an important occasion like the Fourth of July. The family and friends occasion drives the most volume and has the most emotional meaning. When families and friends gather, the harmony metaphor comes into play. Everyone who attends the occasion hopes everyone will get along. Harmony is the aspiration...when grandparents and three-year-olds and everyone else is in harmony.

Potato chips are the world's favorite snack because they connect everyone – a simple pleasure of life that brings everyone together. Hence, potato chips link to the Fundamental Beliefs of potato lovers.

The Desired Target Experience is the feeling of "the kid in all of us." Our potato lovers all picked one image as their favorite. Four little boys in their treehouse pulling up a rope attached to a basket that contained their dog and in the dog's mouth is a bag of potato chips. The target loves the light-hearted humor of the treehouse scene...everyone can relate to the innocent feeling of doing things just for the fun of it. Everyone can relate to that feeling and everyone loves having that feeling.

To potato chip lovers, potato chips strongly link to that feeling. Potato chips are a simple pleasure – maybe the simplest pleasure. And it's the simple pleasures that connect us all, including the somewhat mischievous little boys in the treehouse gathering their potato chips with the help of their dog.

In focus groups with moms of young kids, the moms were shown the treehouse image. They told us the following story. The boys had been told not to eat potato chips between meals. The boys somehow found a way to train the dog to bring the potato chips to the tree house. The boys had found a rather outlandish way to disobey. The lesson for moms. Boys will be boys...thank goodness.

And the potato lovers told us the very best potato chips are light, i.e. their lightness lets each chip melt in your mouth. Salty snacks are, by their nature, irresistible. And the most irresistible chips are the lightest. After we completed the global flat chips Brand Platform, Frito-Lay R&D conducted product tests that taught them that Lays (and other Frito-Lay brands around the world) were not the lightest. R&D spent a year reformulating the potato chip to be the lightest.

Product testing confirmed their success. The Brand Platform was rolled out globally with the reformulated "light" product.

The Brand Concept headline. "The Simple Pleasures of Life"

The Visual. Four little boys in their treehouse

The Unique Advantage and Support: The Light Irresistible Taste of Lays for the Kid in All of Us.

The Brand Concept rationale:

1) Simple Pleasures of Life links to the Harmony metaphor
2) The treehouse visual taps into the mischievous, innocent fun of childhood
3) The Light Irresistible Taste expresses Lay's unique irresistibility vs other potato chips and all other snacks – salty or otherwise.

It's important to note that qualitative research conducted at the Conceptualization Stage is optimization research, i.e. we learn which collection of words and images are most motivating to target consumers. Consumers are usually very clear which words and pictures really motivate them and which do not. Net, net, the process is consumer driven. We use our best judgment to create the strongest Brand Concepts and let the consumer teach us when we have hit the mark.

Another point is worth making. Clients ask us if the images or words we use are advertising. They are not. The Brand Concepts are a vehicle to test a brand hypothesis. They are strategic concepts. They are not "copy." Creativity needs focus. Our Brand Platforms and Brand Concepts are designed to focus the creation of executional elements, e.g. package design, web design, advertising, PR, R&D. Creative people value the Platforms and Concepts because they are very rich in consumer insight and quite different from traditional briefs which tend to be more linear. Imagery in the creative brief is usually considered the most insightful...creative people can "feel" the truth.

Chapter 8

Implementation Stage

Step 8

This stage creates the execution roadmap to bring the Brand Concept to life at all consumer touch points including messaging, paid and earned media, web and package design, activations, social media.

Guidelines are created that include:

- do's and don'ts...what words and images work and don't work communicating the Brand Concept. Clients have told us that do's and don'ts are quite valuable helping organizations implement Brand Platforms. Why an image or collection of words motivates or fails to motivate helps people who were not deeply involved in the brand building process have practical ground rules to apply the learning.

Usually a small core team, maybe 5–10 individuals, is deeply involved in the brand building process. Teams ultimately involved in executing the Platform are much larger and probably were not involved or only peripherally involved. They need clear, concise tools and temples to guide their work. The tools help keep the organization from drifting from the core truths or reinventing them.

It should also be noted that there is usually a person or two who was involved in brand creation who brings continuity to the branding process. Sometimes that person is called "Keeper of the Brand Keys" ...a person who can be consulted when there are questions about how best to execute a particular brand asset.

We also believe that the brand story should be expressed in different ways to help ensure that new people to the branding team internalize the brand truths. We all learn in different ways…by expressing the brand truths in different formats we increase the odds that individuals will find the format that best answers their questions and win their support.

In addition to do's and don'ts, two other tools or formats are Brand Vision and Brand Purpose:

Brand Vision that captures on one page:

- the target insight that inspired the brand positioning. The process will uncover many insights. The Brand Vision template needs to identify the singular insight that underpins the positioning. The global flat chips insight: simple pleasures connect all of us and potato chips are one of life's simple pleasures.
- the positioning statement "answers" the insight…brings the insight to life. The positioning usually combines the Desired Target Experience with the Unique Advantage.

The global flat chips statement is a good example: "the light, irresistible taste of Lay's for the kid in all of us." We want potato chip lovers to have "the kid in all of us" feeling. When they go to the store to buy potato chips, that "feeling" will motivate them to buy Lay's. It's a feeling that links both their Fundamental Belief about connecting us all and why Lay's is the best choice. The "light, irresistible taste of Lay's" supplies the rational reason our potato chips will taste better. The "feeling" is the most important brand asset. Humans cannot make a decision if they don't feel it. It's how we are wired. The feeling transforms Lay's from a functional brand (based on taste alone) to an aspirational brand that links to the target's Beliefs and Desired Experience.

- the key messages that communicate the Brand Concept; what the target will take away from the messages, i.e. what the target will feel, think, and do in response to the messages.

In this section of the Vision, we list the key messages we believe will best motivate potato chip lovers, i.e. the messages that best bring the positioning to life. We also communicate how these messages will make the target feel, think, and do. We can use quantitative research to measure if the target does indeed feel, think, and do what we want it to.

■ the brand/company values and the brand persona. The brand values reflect our beliefs as a company...why we are in business, how we regard the consumers we serve.

The brand persona is designed to bring the brand alive as if they are a person. If the brand were to walk into a room, is the brand a male or female, how old are they, where do they live, what do they do for fun, at a party, how do they behave, how do others react to him or her. Net, net, another tool to tell our brand story.

Creativity needs focus and "stuff." The focus comes from our Brand Platform and Concept. The "stuff" is our imagery, our do's and don'ts, our brand persona.

■ Brand Purpose that expresses how the Brand will change the target's life for the better.

The Brand Purpose should also be created in a work session with the cross-functional marketing team involved in the branding process. Companies have learned that their most valuable brands have a purpose well beyond making a profit contribution. When a brand defines how its consumers' lives will be enhanced, the brand has more meaning, and value and the internal organization feels more fulfilled in their work.

At this point, a decision needs to be taken whether quantitative research is needed to confirm the appeal of the Brand Concept. The brand development process may have produced evidence the Concept is strong and further research is not warranted. On the other hand, the risks associated with launching the Brand may be so high, new data are needed to confirm the opportunity.

PROCESS VALIDATION

Chapter 9

Guiding Principles

- What are the guiding principles that inform the process?
- Creativity needs focus and "stuff." Organizations almost universally have strategy formats to guide branding endeavors. Often these formats focus on "left brain" questions, e.g. the extent and degree of unmet needs, market size and growth, target demos. All the above information is, of course, valuable. What the strategy formats often omit are deep consumer insight to help the creative people and agencies who have to bring the brand to life.
- Our process is designed to focus creative people with insight into the feelings that tell their brand story. The "stuff" is part of the brief – the images that really inspired the target and the story the images tell. Imagery for a long time came into play after the Brand Platform or strategy was developed. Imagery was viewed as an executional element. In our experience, imagery is also a powerful strategic tool. Imagery is universal; words often have a cultural context. Imagery can express emotions that all humans feel. On a related note, we conducted Pampers research in Japan among first time Japanese moms. The source of our imagery was magazines which used western models. The Japanese moms picked an image of a mom embracing her newborn. Both mom and baby were looking into each other's eyes. That image was their favorite because it expressed "skinship" – the emotional and physical bond between mom and child that lasts a lifetime.
- We asked about whether the western model bothered them. They said no because the image reflected "skinship...a universal value." They did

DOI: 10.4324/9781003223313-12

wish the mom in the image was Japanese so they could better read her eyes.

■ Humans are always using their imagination to prospect for a better future. The psychologists who developed the positive psychology theory believe that we humans were misnamed Homo Sapiens. Though it would be nice if humans were universally wise, wisdom is not our strong suit.

■ Their studies suggest we should be named Homo Prospectus. That's because we are always prospecting for a better future. It's our memory and imagination that set us apart from other species.

■ Our nature is to use our imagination to explore future options. We do so for big and small things...when to go shopping...when to change jobs.

■ Ultimately, we decide what future course of action to take. Our branding process applies positive psychology principles. We use imagery to tap into our imagination of what might be. In our case, we study target consumers using imagery to teach us about their desired experiences in life and, more specifically, the experiences that relate to the brand we are developing. We've learned that what people wish for – what they imagine – is a good clue about the kind of future they seek. We want our brand to help them realize that future.

■ Human thought is image-based and two thirds of what we see is behind our eyes. Tacit knowledge is critical to our process. I suspect tacit knowledge is more right-brained (for righthanded people). It's the perceptual mode of the brain. If we need to make a big decision, we often make a list of pluses and minuses – a left-brained exercise using our cognitive power to reason. In the middle of the night, we wake up having made a decision. The left brain has a rather dominant impact on our thinking and usually overrules the right brain or, more to the point, doesn't let it operate.

■ Some psychologists believe that once we developed the capacity for language which names and labels things, we gave the left brain the power to run the show. When we woke up in the middle of the night with our decision, the left brain was asleep. The right brain is now free to reign – a chance to review the previous day and "think" about the things we haven't yet resolved. In my own experience, I've gone to sleep with unresolved issues and awakened with a solution that had not occurred to me before I went to bed. I suspect the right brain/perceptual mode is in charge of my thinking.

■ We humans "feel" what we want to do. We "feel" the decision that we make. We are not capable of making a decision unless we feel it. Our brain has evolved to include cognitive reasoning skills with the power of decision making residing in the emotional or limbic part of our brain.

■ Imagery helps make tacit knowledge explicit so it can be addressed. We think in images. And we have memories to shape our thinking. To exemplify, we have an image of a boy on a mountain bike at the top of a cliff. When we show the image to boys who love mountain biking, all they feel is an adrenaline rush...going off that cliff without knowing the consequences.

■ When we show the same image to their mothers, all they feel is fear and danger. Two thirds of what we see is behind our eyes.

■ Complex problems should be broken down into discreet elements before integrating into a holistic solution. One of the biggest barriers to creating a brand concept is the desire to "leap it"...to conceptualize all the elements of the concept. This approach is not very productive because we don't know enough about the elements of the concept to put all the pieces together. We've learned a better approach is to identify the elements of a concept and first understand each element, and then let the target consumer put all the elements together into a holistic solution.

■ The four elements of a Brand Platform are Beliefs, Desired Experiences, Unique Advantage, and Unique Advantage Support. Our process lets the consumer teach us about each element individually. And then lets the consumer build the links between each element. The consumer is very clear in their understanding of how the elements link together in their mind. And it's their linkage that matters. In sum, leaping to the solution is often counterproductive and in the end a time waster. Let the consumer teach you about concept elements and how they tie together to get you there faster and with a much stronger brand story.

■ The wider and deeper the framework, the greater the odds of a big idea. I'm not sure where I first heard that idea, but when I did hear it, it made intuitive sense. The Business Framework, the Brand Platform, the strategic use of imagery, are all a response to that principle.

  – On a related note, I remember reading Michael Porter's book Competitive Strategy. The gist of what I learned...my conception of the competitive landscape was way too narrow. When I embraced his much wider lens...embracing all buyers and suppliers in the value chain, emerging technology et al.…my mind was open to much more powerful ways to compete.

■ "People don't value what they don't create." My P&G client developed that principle. We had worked together with P&G's Far East Division to create the Pampers Brand Platform. Unfortunately, P&G's other divisions did not go along with us on the journey. And, as a result, they didn't believe our results. As a consequence, each division redid our Far East work to decide if they should believe us. P&G lost four years getting to market with the new Brand Platform. If people are involved in the process, their questions answered, their ideas considered, they feel they are on the team and part of the solution.

■ "Culture eats strategy for breakfast." I've heard many definitions of corporate culture. The definition that's most meaningful to me: corporate culture codifies the philosophy and practices that underpin a company's success. A few tenets of a company's culture help demonstrate the definition. Walmart believes that they are master or merchandising and their suppliers are the master of the consumer. Suppliers who teach Walmart about the consumer are highly valued. Walmart seeks to partner with these suppliers to grow markets and lead with product innovations. Walmart highly values its flexible distribution system. Even though Walmart is bigger than Africa, it moves like a startup to change merchandise aisles. Walmart was able to dethrone Toys R Us as the toy leader in a few weeks because the company could in a matter of weeks go from two aisles to five aisles of toys for the six weeks before Christmas. Other retailers need 6–12 months to make a similar move.

■ Amazon is fiercely focused on consumer satisfaction. Consumers value that focus and believe it separates Amazon from most other retailers… all of whom are now attempting to catch up. P&G believes consumer insight is key…if employees don't have good insight, their projects aren't funded. The company believes that R&D is the key to driving long-term growth. They invest more in R&D than their competitors in both basic and applied research. P&G also believes that a product concept must enjoy a significant win in quantitative research. The product concept must be functionally driven to be meaningful and measurable. That cultural belief was a barrier to success with Pampers. P&G had to learn a new approach to success…in this case the lessons learned from our project. The P&G culture needed to reflect this new truth. Fortunately, the company has executives who have been designated thought leaders to help the company ensure that its culture isn't a slave to the past.

If culture codifies success, the factors that comprise success must be updated, reflecting marketing and technology changes.

■ You can't teach anyone anything until you understand the concepts in their head. A professor of education taught me this lesson. His specialty was childhood education. His insight: you can't teach a three-year-old about water until you first learn about the concepts in the child's head about water. Once you understand the child's concepts, you can introduce your new concepts about water. Assuming you do this well, the child will learn how your concepts link to his in going understanding. Teaching isn't learning and learning isn't teaching.

■ On a broader level, helping people make behavioral changes is very difficult, e.g. to stop smoking. People need to see and believe in the benefits of not smoking on their own terms or behavioral change will not take place. A classic example...advertising was created that pictured diseased lungs that result from smoking. The effect on teenage smoking: no change. Another ad was created picturing a teenage boy with yellowed fingers from smoking and a teenage girl rejecting him as gross. The result: teenage smoking declined.

■ Humans can't make a decision unless they "feel it." Antonio Damasio's book, *Descartes' Error*, teaches us why. Damasio is a neuroscientist who studied patients with damage to the portion of their brain that controls our "feelings" ...usually the right brain in righthanded people. These people had all their left-brain capacities intact...they were highly logical and could engage in endless discussions about strengths and weaknesses of an idea. What they could not do was make a decision about anything. The reason: our decision-making capabilities are wired to our limbic system which evolved from our brain stem and was in place before our cognitive mental capacity. So to make a decision, our limbic system is mandatory. Descartes was incorrect when he famously said:

■ "I think therefore I am." We are the result of the beliefs we hold and the decisions we make with regard to those beliefs. We are mostly unaware or not actively conscious of our limbic system consciousness...beyond survival instincts such as fight or flight. Descartes lived during the Enlightenment era and deeply valued rational thought and the scientific method. Humans are at their finest when they engage in rational thinking...I think therefore I am. Descartes believed that rational thought should rule our lower or base emotions which are a residue of our animal past...before we had evolved to become human.

- The truth about us humans is more complicated. Corporate culture, religion, political beliefs, myths have a powerful impact on who we are. They are not reducible to rational argument but to emotions and feelings. The branding process seeks to embrace where decisions are made and what motivates us to make them.

- Damasio helped us get a handle on how our mind works and what consciousness is all about.

- Analogies, archetypes, and metaphors inspire creativity. We find analogies instructive. The potato chip market is like the cola market. That analogy helped us reimagine the potato chip category. It was seen as a commodity market comprising "me too" brands where changes in market share were based on retail prices. The cola analogy suggested that if potato chips could behave like cola brands, they would no longer be a commodity but deliver branded value and pricing. The analogy was a mind opener that set the brand building process in motion.

- Archetypes have a different role in brand building. They are useful in developing brand persona. Is our brand a Warrior, Magician, Jester, Lover, Innocent. All I know is that the people in our lives…friends and family…celebrities…tend to exhibit archetype personality traits. Examining an array of archetypes helps us think through the personal qualities of our brand. The result: another way to bring our brand to life for consumers and the internal organization.

- Metaphors are the most powerful tool for brand creation. Potato Chips are Harmony…the simple pleasures that connect us all. Pampers are healthy growth and development. Godiva is passion. Minivans are a hug for your kids. If you can find the right metaphor, you will never think of your brand the same way…the metaphor will define your brand essence. Metaphors are the way humans describe the world.

- Lakoff and Johnson's book, *Metaphors We Live By*, teaches us that metaphorical concepts organize our thinking and how we see and describe our world. Metaphors such as Argument is War, Food is Love, and Time is Money are not just about language but how we experience and act in the world. When Shakespeare's "All the world's a stage" or Thomas More is "lion in winter" give us a way of thinking about experience and behaving. The irony is that we are hardly aware of the profound power of metaphor. And when we are, we tend to think of metaphors as poetic or literary devices. Even the two basic modes of thinking are impacted by metaphor. Rational thinking is up and emotions are down. With rational thinking, we exercise our control over the universe. With emotions we show our "lower" nature...our similarity to animals. These metaphors influence our thinking in ways we are not really aware of... and they hide us from the truth. In this case, a narrow, incorrect view of human consciousness.

■ Our opportunity is to develop the metaphor that will communicate a powerful brand story.

Chapter 10

Academic Underpinnings

What academic research informs the process?

Readers who want to deepen their understanding of academic research that supports the Success Model and Method will want to explore the books below.

- *Descartes' Error* by Antonio Damasio. Humans can only make decisions with their feelings. The limbic system rules. It's not "I think therefore I am." It's "I am, therefore I think." How our mind actually works. What consciousness is really all about...cognitive and perceptual processes.
- *Homo Prospectus* by Martin Seligman. Humans are always using their imagination to explore better futures.
- *The Hero Within* by Carol Pearson. How to tap the power of archetypes. Carl Jung made accessible and valuable.
- *The Hero with a Thousand Faces* by Joseph Campbell. The monomyth created by all societies and cultures...the hero's journey accepting his call to action to move from the known to the unknown world ultimately transforming himself and those around him.
- *Sapiens: A Brief History of Humankind* by Yuval Noah Harari. Creating the beliefs that motivated humans to trust people beyond their immediate hunter gatherer family.
- *Drawing on the Right Side of the Brain* by Betty Edwards. The power of perception housed in our right brain which the logical, left brain wants to suppress.
- *Reality Is Broken: Why Games Make Us Better and How They Can Change the World* by Jane McGonigal, explaining the psychological underpinnings of games.

DOI: 10.4324/9781003223313-13

- *Metaphors We Live By* by George Lakoff and Mark Johnson. How metaphors structure the way we think, experience life and create.
- *Catching Fire. How Cooking Made Us Human* by Richard Wrangham. We are what we eat applied to ancient hunter gatherers...our digestive systems, our connections with each other around the campfire.
- *Two Cultures and the Scientific Revolution* by C. P. Snow. Intellectual life in western society was split into two cultures...science and the humanities. The division is a significant barrier to solving the world's problems.

Chapter 11

Culture and Fundamental Human Beliefs

Fundamental Human Beliefs are above culture. So what role does culture play in the branding process? Culture is a difficult subject to tackle. There is the dominant culture of a country; the cultural imperative of the United States is "to do," the UK, "to be," France, "to think," Japan, "to obey." If the brand we are developing is to be marketed in any of those four countries, we'd want to be sure we express our Brand Concept in a way that reflects the cultural imperative of a given country. The Fundamental Human Belief, for discussion's sake, is Connections, the connections between friends and family that give life meaning. The Belief needs to be expressed in a way that conforms with cultural imperatives. I should note that a global brand concept can be expressed in a way that all countries and cultures can relate to.

On another level, many cultural values are always in flux...our beliefs about material possessions (bigger is better), sexual mores, life's journey, gender identity, making a contribution to make the world a better place. Generation after generation seeks to express its way of living the best, happiest, most fulfilling life.

Fundamental Human Beliefs are above cultural values...Beliefs about Belonging, Mission, Identity, Capabilities are universal and we define ourselves against those Beliefs. Brands tied to those Beliefs are, as such, more meaningful to us. We need to be aware of culture and be sensitive to what culture suggests about communicating our Brand Platform.

DOI: 10.4324/9781003223313-14

CASE HISTORIES

Chapter 12

Pampers

What Can the Pampers Case Teach Us about the Process?

Situation. Procter & Gamble launched Pampers into an Indianapolis test market in the early 1950s. The brand was unsuccessful for close to a decade despite many efforts to improve performance including new packaging and pricing.

Research was conducted to understand what was holding moms back from buying. The problem was the moms' moms. Grandmothers wanted their glorious grandchildren in cloth diapers. Their daughters were not to take the lazy way out with "paper" diapers. They were to go to the laundry room and wash the cloth diapers.

P&G's response was research that proved that Pampers kept babies drier than cloth diapers. New moms could now explain that Pampers was better for the baby than cloth diapers.

"Keeps babies drier" became the Pampers slogan. The disposable diaper market exploded and Pampers had a 100% share. Potential new competitors took notice; premium brands like Huggies in the United States and Unicharm in Japan and private label manufacturers all wanted in on the action. The price of entry; promise to keep babies drier. The result was Pampers' share declined over the years to 30% and stayed at that level for 10 years despite many efforts to develop product benefits that would give Pampers a competitive advantage. Net, net, Pampers' "keep babies drier" benefit had created the market but, in time, became a generic benefit in a commoditized market.

DOI: 10.4324/9781003223313-16

Challenge. Apply our branding process with the goal to regain growing global leadership for Pampers.

Solution. P&G wanted to apply the brand building process in Japan. It was their belief that the Japanese consumer was much more precise than consumers in the rest of the world. If the challenge could be solved in Japan, the rest of the world would follow.

The core target was first time moms who are anxious about motherhood and want to do everything they can for their new baby. Their Fundamental Human Belief was "skinship"…

the physical and emotional bond between mother and child that will last a lifetime.

Their Desired Target Experience was a comfortable feeling when mother and baby are relaxed and happy together…the feeling that creates the best experience for building the bonds of skinship.

The skinship belief and the comfortable feeling is all about the target's life and is independent of the brand.

Pampers Unique Advantage was developed by having first time moms evaluate an array of brand hypotheses with the potential to create a unique competitive advantage. One benefit was favored over all the others: supporting babies' healthy growth and development. The moms told us that Pampers did not deliver that benefit today but if it could, Pampers would become their preferred brand.

The next step in the process was to explore how Pampers could deliver healthy growth and development. The solution was to develop a Pampers diaper for each stage in the baby's development. The moms felt that their baby had different diaper requirements at each stage i.e. newborns needed to feel extra comforted (the diaper should feel like an external womb), the next stage needed to support a baby's movement. Swaddlers for newborns and Cruisers for the infant and toddler stages.

The moms could now tell a holistic story…Pampers Stages help moms support a baby's healthy growth and development which enables the moms to experience the comfortable, loving feeling that links to skinship…her Fundamental Human Belief.

Results. The reinvented Pampers was relaunched globally and within four years the Brand's revenue grew from a decade of flat sales at $3B to $12B globally. Pampers Brand Purpose which was once a functional benefit of "keeping babies drier" was now an aspirational benefit that changes mom's life for better. The Brand was reframed in the target's mind as unique…"different in kind" vs competition.

Chapter 13

Lays

What Can the Global Flat Chips Case Teach Us about the Process?

Situation. Frito-Lay decided to expand globally via acquisition. The company's strategy was to buy one of the leading snack food companies in each expansion country. Once the acquisitions were completed, Frito-Lay's growth strategy was to launch proprietary US brands into each international market to drive growth. Ruffles was the first brand to be introduced internationally. Ruffles grew rapidly behind strong introductory marketing support, but subsequently declined when the support was withdrawn. Frito-Lays concluded that their growth strategy was a failure.

Over the next several months, marketing management developed a new growth strategy hypothesis. Potato chips were far and away the largest snack food category and potato chips were everyone's favorite snack. Potato chips (in the company's jargon, potato chips are known as flat chips), were viewed and managed as a commodity. Whichever brand of chips was on sale at the supermarket was the best seller of the week. In the United States, Frito-Lay would promote Lays one year and Ruffles the next. Whichever brand was priced lowest, sold the most.

Within the Frito-Lay portfolio, potato chips' role was to "anchor" retail space while the high profit snacks like Doritos and Tostitos drove profitable volume growth.

The new growth strategy hypothesis: Is it possible to create a global brand platform for flat chips that would establish a unique competitive advantage for Frito-Lay potato chip brands and justify premium pricing?

DOI: 10.4324/9781003223313-17

To test the hypothesis, the first step was to conduct Marketplace P&L studies in all Frito-Lay countries. The studies would teach us whether the market structure for all snacks varied by market, whether potato chips were the favorite snack in each market and the perception of the potato chip category. The studies concluded that potato chips were the favorite snack everywhere. The implication: if a global brand platform could be created, the platform could be implemented successfully in each country.

Frito-Lay's international management team felt that Marketplace P&L studies would help ensure each country's marketing team would buy into the global growth strategy. Before the studies, country managers felt that their country's potato chip market had unique characteristics. The studies proved otherwise.

The hypothesis was named the "cola of chips." Data from cola markets around the world show that the larger the cola market in each country, the larger the total soft drink market. If potato chips could be marketed and managed like colas, could we expect similar results?

Challenge. Develop the global brand platform for flat chips that will be emotionally engaging and create premium value. The platform will be applied for each country brand, i.e. Lays in the US, Walkers in the UK, Matutano in Spain, Sabritas in Mexico.

Solution. Research was undertaken in several countries including the US, Spain, UK, Mexico and Brazil where Frito-Lay had a potato chip brand. Research was also conducted in China where there were no potato chips (and no potatoes).

Everyone eats potato chips so the research design included teens, moms and dads, and grandparents.

The Global Flat Chips Brand Platform

Fundamental Human Belief is Harmony...the simple pleasures that connect us all.

Desired Consumer Experience..."the kid in all of us" feeling

The Unique Advantage is Irresistible. It's the generic benefit of all snacks. Potato chips, as the world's favorite snack, have more of a right to own Irresistible. To move Frito-Lays potato chip brands from being a branded commodity to a premium brand, the platform needed to find a way to "brand" the generic benefit of Irresistible (much as Tide needed to brand the generic benefit of detergents, i.e. Clean).

The Unique Advantage Support... the light, crispy taste.

Results. The global brand platform was executed first in packaging with a "banner sun" icon communicating a feeling of harmony in sunny yellow colors. For low margin categories like potato chips, packaging is the dominant media budget. The package told the platform story via design.

Advertising was created against the brief: "the kid in all of us". Lighted hearted and fun commercials were created that drove sales and justified premium pricing.

Chapter 14

Disney

What Can the Disney Boys Brand Platform Teach Us about the Process?

Situation. The Disney Channel was highly successful building a bond with kids and preteen girls. Boys were often in the audience but were mostly watching to find out what girls are all about. Disney had acquired the Power Rangers property which attracted boys but was ultimately sold because it did not fit the Disney brand equity. Disney needed to develop a TV brand that would fit Disney equity and win with boys.

Challenge. Develop a Global Brand Platform for boys. Assuming success, the platform would become a way for Disney to chat with boys on a regular basis and be a gateway to franchising, i.e. Disney movies, theme parks, consumer products.

Solution. The target audience are boys ages 6–12.

The Fundamental Human Belief is Accomplishment. Boys love their buddies and want to be with them through thick and thin.

But on an individual or personal level, boys want to be able to do things and do them well. At ages 6–12 their opportunity might be accomplished in a variety of ways, e.g. athletics, music, gaming, science…more or less a metaphor for the accomplishment they seek when they are grown up.

The Desired Target Experience is feeling "Unstoppable"…that feeling inside us when we know we can do something that we value. I'm reminded of the scene in the Bad News Bears when the team had finally started to win and they were about to play the big game. The look on their faces said

DOI: 10.4324/9781003223313-18

they feel "unstoppable"...even before the game, they knew they were ready. They'd overcome fear and doubt...they expected good things to happen.

The Accomplishment belief linked to the Unstoppable feeling reflects the boys' aspirations in life.

The Unique Advantage of the boys' TV channel is to "discover who they are and who they want to be." The channel should tell stories in the spirit of The Hero's Journey where boys accept the call to adventure, go from the known to the unknown world, transform themselves, and ultimately us. As one example, the *Phineas and Ferb* show was quite perfect for the new boys' channel.

Results. The new boys' channel was named Disney XD. Disney reflects the master brand values and XD signals a new direction for boys (girls were invited) and different from the Disney Channel. Disney XD was a successful addition to the Disney TV portfolio. Disney subsequently acquired the *Star Wars* and *Marvel* properties that added value to the total Disney franchise overall and, importantly, boys.

Chapter 15

Godiva

What Can the Godiva Case Teach Us about the Process?

Situation. After decades of double digit growth, Godiva sales flattened and then declined. The brand's franchise was aging and the brand's image was less appealing. Godiva was seen as a good corporate gift, i.e. an executive's gift to an assistant at Christmas.

Godiva was losing at the entry point, i.e. the brand had not attracted a generation of younger chocolate lovers.

Challenge. Drive Godiva growth by reinventing the brand to attract a younger cohort without losing the older loyalists.

Solution. To younger chocolate lovers, chocolate is passion. Their Desired Experience was a feeling of passion which they link to chocolate and the loving relationships they seek in life. Godiva's positioning was recast to communicate a feeling of passion. The Brand expressed the passion messaging, product innovation, the indulgent in store experience. The Lady Godiva icon had been Lady Godiva herself in a suit of armor. Her armor was removed and she was now nude as she rode her horse into town as per the original legend.

Results. Godiva became a growth brand again and much of that growth came from winning at the entry point...the younger generation had been won over.

DOI: 10.4324/9781003223313-19

Chapter 16

ABC News

What Can ABC News Teach Us about the Process?

Situation and Challenge. ABC News wanted to develop a Brand Positioning Concept, Tagline, Mission, and Values Statements that would give them competitive advantage vs CBS News and NBC News. At the time, NBC News was the ratings leader.

Solution. The target, news involved consumers, wanted "big picture" insight from news to help them make better life decisions. ABC News translated that insight into external and internal messaging.

The ABC News campaign tagline: *"See the Whole Picture"*

The Organization Mission: To inform, inspire and empower people so they can better understand the world and change the future.

ABC News Values:

- Compelling and accurate journalism – and emotionally engaging non-fiction storytelling – is what we do.
- We relentlessly pursue the truth, independently, without fear or favor.
- We are passionate and deeply curious about the world.
- Creativity and innovation are key to our growth.
- We win as a team.
- Our strength comes from our diversity – in our backgrounds, perspectives, audiences, people, and choices
- We are a multi-platform service. We are always on…delivering Information when, where, and how our users need it.

DOI: 10.4324/9781003223313-20

Results. ABC News, relaunched with the new brand story, became the ratings leader within 2 years and remains so today. The Mission and Values Statements focused and motivated ABC News people to deliver the *See the Whole Picture* promise.

Chapter 17

Ore Ida

What Can Ore Ida Teach Us about the Process?

Situation. Ore Ida was the mainstream leader of the retail frozen french fries market. The brand was built on two pillars: (1) Ore Ida was "baked, not fried," which made the buyer feel better about serving them, and (2) Ore Ida Tater Tots which kids and most everyone else loved. Tater Tots were made from the leftover potato scraps after potatoes were sliced into french fries prior to cooking. From a cost of goods standpoint, the total Ore Ida line was much more profitable than frozen food in general because of the high utilization of raw (potato) material. The brand controlled about 50% of the market; Ore Ida sales would show modest growth when the price differential between Ore Ida and private label competition was modest and sales would decline if the differential was pushed too high.

The total frozen french fry market and Ore-Ida sales flattened out. Heinz management became disillusioned with the potato category. On the executive floor in Pittsburgh was heard: "potatoes are history."

Challenge. Develop an Ore Ida Brand Growth Strategy that will make the Brand a positive contributor to Heinz corporate earnings.

Solution. Mom was the primary buyer of frozen french fries. When she married, her dream was family dinners with her husband and kids chatting about their day. Moms selected an image of the family dinner which showed the whole family with smiles on their faces...Mom's most desired experience. The reality at dinner time was often marked by sibling fights...very far from her aspiration.

DOI: 10.4324/9781003223313-21

Mom's Fundamental Belief was her mission to raise her kids right. The Desired Experience was a "feeling" of closeness with her kids...a signal she was doing the right things by them. Ore Ida's Unique Advantage was helping mom serve happy and wholesome meals.

The Brand Platform was translated into advertising that showed mom's busy life ending in a meal served with that included Ore Ida fries. Most importantly the whole family was together and happy. Ore Ida was the difference maker. Fries on the plate often resulted in kids asking mom: "Have we been good today?" The advertising linked to mom's aspiration for her role as nurturer. Ore Ida honored mom.

Results. Ore Ida reversed its sales decline, sourcing volume from moms who were medium to heavy category users, i.e. drove category volume and profits. These moms increased the number of Ore Ida occasions. Importantly, Ore Ida's marketing budget was increased above the line (advertising) and decreased below the line (price promotion) with no change in overall budget size. Whenever a brand can effectively spend more dollars above the line, they build long-term value. Brands forced to increase below the line dollars are competing on price and not building equity.

Chapter 18

ASU

What Can Arizona State University Teach Us about the Process?

Situation. Michael Crow, the President of ASU for the past 17 years is transforming public education with a vision to enable students to have a more fulfilling experience in school and throughout the course of their lives. About 100,000 students attend school on campus. Another 50,000 attend ASU online. The online university is much more profitable than the bricks and mortar campus.

Challenge. Develop the Brand Platform to create Unique Advantage for ASUOnline vs current and emerging competition. For profit universities started online education. Their offering was often not of good quality and students in many cases felt they were being ripped off. A few universities including ASU wanted to improve the perception of the category by offering a quality experience that students really valued.

At the time our project was initiated, ASUO was a success. The issue going forward was that many prestigious universities now wanted to participate in the online market and were initiating or expanding their online programs. The desired outcome of the project: (1) a deep emotional bond with current, prospective, and alumni of ASUO and (2) higher enrollment.

Two barriers to success: (1) the way ASUO (and competitors) went to market. As a public university, ASU's budget needed to be approved by the state government. State governments were always under budget pressure. (2) University cultures are anti-marketing. Academics believe the idea of investing tens of millions of dollars to attract students is sinful. That same money

DOI: 10.4324/9781003223313-22

could attract better faculty and support academic research to grow knowledge. The solution was to partner with those parties with the digital marketing skills to drive enrollment. The third parties would make the marketing investment, not ASU. ASU would split the revenue. ASUO increased enrollment without having to make an upfront investment.

The problem with that arrangement was that the third party focused every marketing dollar, pushing prospects to enroll and zero dollars building the ASUO brand.

Solution. The core prospects for online education are "life first, school second" students. Their average age was early thirties, they often were married with kids. They were ambitious people who knew the value of a degree to advance their career and make their life more fulfilling. They were for the most part not natural students, may have had difficulty in school, were time and financially constrained.

Their Fundamental Belief was Fulfillment that comes from doing everything they can to improve their life and the life of their family. Their Desired Experience, to feel empowered. The Unique Advantage is ASUO's dedication to each student's success. Being remote online…feeling unsupported… feeling lost in a big university…is their fear.

ASUO, by contrast, has put in place the academic, financial, social, and psychological resources and success coaches to exceed student expectations and bring to life ASU's dedication to each student in school and over the course of their lives

Results. It's early on but initial results are encouraging. Enrollments are up in 2021 despite the pandemic which has had a negative impact on university attendance broadly.

Chapter 19

Dodge

What Can Dodge Teach Us about the Process?

Situation. Chrysler invented the minivan category with the Dodge Caravan the dominant leader and Chrysler Town and Country building the premium segment. Minivans sold a million vehicles annually several years post launch. And then came SUVs. SUVs effectively positioned minivans as a mom mobile. Cool moms wanted the adventurous image of an off-road vehicle. Minivan sales softened.

    Challenge. Develop a Brand Platform for Dodge Caravan that will drive category and brand growth.

    Solution. Target buyers/drivers were families with several young kids. Some of the target consumers owned a minivan so the mission was to motivate them to make their next vehicle a minivan. Other families in the target market did not own a minivan so our Brand Platform was to bring them into the category. Within the family market target, mom was key.

> The Fundamental Belief that motivated moms (and dads) was Connection...a close and connected family.
> The Desired Experience was feeling appreciated for creating a loving environment for the family.
> The Unique Advantage...driving a Dodge Caravan was like giving your family a hug every time you went for a ride.
> The Unique Advantage Support...among many features, room for everyone and everything...each child had his or her own bucket seat...great visibility.

DOI: 10.4324/9781003223313-23

Results. Dodge Caravan sales stabilized and began to grow. The image appeal of SUVs is powerful. But to the segments of moms to whom nurturing their kids was paramount, Dodge Caravan now had a Brand Platform that made its case in highly emotional and inspirational terms.

At a higher level, the Dodge Caravan story is a good example of marketing to strength. It was no accident that minivans became a huge category. The SUV story made minivans culturally less important. The key for Dodge was to find a way to tell their story in a way that honored mom and gave her the arguments she needed to justify her decision.

Another important and more general point: the market target for many brands and categories may hold the same Fundamental Belief, e.g. Connection or Belonging. Building a Brand Platform needs to be grounded in the Beliefs the target lives by. The Desired Experience, i.e. the singular feeling that links to both that Belief and the Unique Advantage is the secret sauce of the Platform. The feeling...expressed in imagery and words...is what unlocks the key to the Success Model. If that feeling is effectively communicated, the target will be honored, the brand will build a deep emotional bond with the target, and the brand will be insulated from competition.

Chapter 20

Lagunitas

What Can Lagunitas Teach Us about the Brand Building Process?

Situation. Lager has been the dominant style of beer since the Middle Ages. British brewers in the mid-1700s were asked to add hops to the beers to safeguard them from spoilage during long seafaring journeys to the Caribbean and India. A British journal mentioned India Pale Ale for the first time in 1835. Cut to the mid-1990s in California when a brewer formulated an IPA that introduced the style to local beer drinkers.

Around this time Tony Magee was experimenting with beer making using a home brewer kit his brother had given him. Tony's first brew tasted awful, his follow-on efforts were better...the important point was that he was hooked. He'd found his passion. The Lagunitas Brewing Company was formed in short order. Lagunitas was the California town where his first brewery was located.

Several brewers were making IPAs...a hoppier, somewhat higher alcohol level with a rich combination of bitter and sweet flavor notes vis-à-vis lagers. The new style was gaining fans quickly. Tony's vision was for Lagunitas to own the IPA category. His success would correlate with the growth of the IPA category.

Challenge. To develop the Brand Platform that would establish Lagunitas as the mainstream category leader.

Solution. Beer is Connection. "Let's go have a beer"...beer is a social lubricant...mostly for men but increasingly for women. Many mainstream leaders "own" the key category benefit...the way Tide owns clean. So

DOI: 10.4324/9781003223313-24

Connection was the Fundamental Belief Lagunitas needed to stand for in the minds of prospects...beer lovers looking to discover a more interesting style of beer.

Beer prospects cherish the feeling when they can most be themselves with others...be they old friends or new. They select images that depict relationships with people who "reflect who I am and who appreciate me." Images of people having "fun with life and each other...being completely goofy in a way you can only be with the people you're most comfortable with."

Lagunitas linked to that "just be myself" feeling because every point of contact with the Brand said: "If you could only hang out with one beer, this is the one you would hang out with." The perfect Brand Persona.

"I don't like hanging out with people who are really full of themselves or pretentious. Lagunitas is the opposite of that. It's a beer snob's beer without the snobbishness."

The Lagunitas Unique Advantage is making everyone feel welcome. The beer itself is the most approachable IPA. The pricing is premium but accessible. Most importantly, the Brand's package design and storytelling conveys the personality of a fun loving, somewhat irreverent, don't take life too seriously that attracts everyone...a guy in a suit and a guy with piercings all over himself. Beer drinkers see many breweries as "marketing to the lowest common denominator." They see Lagunitas brewers as having a passion for beer and brewing what they like...hoping the drinkers will enjoy the beer as much as the brewers do. The Lagunitas sales force is a key brand asset. The sales force relationship with distributors, bars, and restaurants is open, helpful, and never bossy...the opposite of the large brewers. The trade looks forward to meeting with Lagunitas people. The sales force never says "please" only "thank you."

Results. Lagunitas has maintained mainstream IPA leadership on a national basis for over a decade. The Brand has grown faster than the IPA category and has helped the IPA category become a core beer style.

A beer drinker summed it up. "Lagunitas is the Bud of IPAs."

Chapter 21

Visa/L'Oreal/Budweiser

All the case histories cited in this book are based on projects with my client except the three I want to share with you now...Visa, L'Oreal, and Budweiser. All three fit the Success Model perfectly. All the case studies in this book are designed to bring the Success Model to life in a variety of different contexts. My hope is that they will help you better understand the Model and believe in its power for brand building. I also hope the particulars of a given case might be relevant to the brand you are taking through the process.

Visa

The credit card market was emerging. Cash and checks were still king. Visa was a local west coast brand and MasterCard was the dominant brand. MasterCard's tagline was spot on: "So Worldly. So Welcome." It signaled that most merchants would accept or "welcome" the card.

It also signaled that the cardholder would be seen as sophisticated or "worldly." The MasterCard positioning was doing its job of growing the credit card market, giving MasterCard leadership credentials and honoring the target prospects for their worldliness.

Then for some unknown reason MasterCard decided to abandon its tagline. That brought cheers of joy at Visa's west coast headquarters. Within a very short time, Visa launched a new positioning and tagline: "Visa, Everywhere you want to be."

DOI: 10.4324/9781003223313-25

Visa's core prospects were early 20-somethings just starting out in life. Their jobs were often rather menial and if they were to use a credit card, it would probably be for mundane things.

Visa advertising focused on beautiful places the target hoped to visit... Carmel, California...Positano, Italy. The card itself was named Visa and the icon suggested global.

The "everywhere" word in the tagline suggested Visa would be accepted everywhere...which is the generic benefit of mainstream credit cards. The "you want to be " said to the 20-something target you have places to go and people to meet...exciting life prospects. Within 10 years, Visa was the global market leader with a 150 million card advantage over MasterCard.

L'Oreal

L'Oreal was competing with mainstream brands like Cover Girl. Their challenge was to justify why the brand should sell at a premium to mainstream brands. The insight that cracked the code: women believed that everyone in the family came before they did. They were raised to sacrifice their needs to the needs of others. L'Oréal changed that female psychology with the tagline: "Because I'm Worth It." L'Oréal was the brand for women who had confidence in their own self-worth and believed that in no way were they to sacrifice their own needs.

Years after L'Oréal launched the positioning, women would tell a different story, i.e. I need to take care of myself first so I can better take care of others. L'Oréal esteemed women. The Brand became a symbol of high self-regard. L'Oréal transformed the way women thought of themselves and clearly justified premium pricing.

Budweiser

When beer was almost exclusively a blue-collar category, Bud was the king of beers.

The campaign that established their leadership was not about the beer but about their drinkers. "This Buds for You for All that You Do." The drinker was honored for all the hard work they do to take care of their families. That tagline is the classic example of the Success Model in action.

EXECUTIVE INTERVIEWS V

Chapter 22

What My Clients
Can Teach Us

And now a word from my clients. My entire career has been on the "sell side." As such, I never had the "buy side" experience of my clients. I would lead a brand building project and do so in a way that encouraged engagement and collaboration with my client team. But at the end of the day, the client had to take ownership of the brand platform and ensure it was effectively implemented long after the project was completed.

I decided to approach my clients and ask them to be interviewed for the book. My hope is that they would give the reader the "buy side" perspective...to understand their view of the brand building process. Net, net, a wider, deeper overview of corporate brand building.

DOI: 10.4324/9781003223313-27

What My Clients Can Teach Us

Chapter 23

Susan Sanderson-Briggs

Susan Sanderson-Briggs. Senior Vice President. Brand Marketing Party City. Formerly SVP Brand and Customer Experience Officer at The Vitamin Shoppe, Director of Corporate Brands at Kroger, VP Group Creative Director at Target.

Susan is an expert at retail reinvention. In most retail organizations, the culture values operational effectiveness far and away above every other capability. Brand strategy is not valued and is often seen as "decoration"... repackaging to sell more effectively. Branding is not viewed as a growth driver.

For branding to win in such environments, it must be presented in terms operating people will understand and value. It must be digestible, tangible, and galvanize an organization to act. Susan sees herself as the Magician archetype...to show people what is possible in terms they comprehend with the end goal to have the people decide to act...they see the truth, believe in it, and act to implement it.

Susan teaches a retail organization a different way of operating. Branding is cloaked in operational language. Be obsessed with the customer or shopper vs an obsession with margin rate or Ebata. It is key that the reinvention is top down...everyone at every level must be involved.

Senior management, salespeople, the stockroom. It's easier to implement branding in specialty retail, e.g. Lululemon, given the focus on a particular segment vs mass retail where the target is exceedingly broad. And every detail matters.

At Vitamin Shoppe, associates are named Health Enthusiasts to reinforce their role with customers and the company's brand essence. Salespeople

DOI: 10.4324/9781003223313-28

felt proud to be called Health Enthusiasts...you could see in their body language...and the feeling projected to the customer. Net, net, customer focused brand platform translated into operational language that was central to the culture and how the retailer succeeded.

I worked with Susan when she was Director of Corporate Brands at Kroger. Kroger's goal was to capture a greater share of their customer's grocery dollars. The company had an excellent database of their customers' buying behavior...it captured every purchase of every item by every customer. A customer segmentation based on the data helped us define the core segment we should focus upon...the "all American families" who drove more than 60% of Kroger's total sales and slightly greater percentage of Kroger's private label brands.

The "all American families" segment did virtually all their grocery shopping with brands that delivered excellent value and low prices...Walmart, Costco, Trader Joe's, and Kroger. The traditional strategy for private label brands was to mimic national brands like Oreos at a lower price.

The project was to determine if there was a better Brand Platform for Kroger's private label products. It's worth noting that Kroger sold more than 5000 P/L products half of which were manufactured by Kroger and the rest sourced from a variety of suppliers with the skill to manufacture products at scale very inexpensively. If Kroger could create a P/L brand that was unique and superior, i.e., reinvent P/L to deliver proprietary value vs the traditional "me too" products at a cheaper price, Kroger would be able to deepen customer loyalty and win a greater share of their grocery dollars.

The core target valued "Connections" with their family – the Fundamental Human Belief that drove their behavior. They selected an image of a family on a swing with mom, dad, and their two kids – their eyes and bodies connected in a mutually loving moment.

Their Desired Experience projected an energized feeling. The image selected was a family jogging on a beach. The story the image told – Connections happen most often when the whole family has the pep and energy to invest in the relationship. The family may value Connections but if one or more family members are tired, the Connection feeling is less likely to happen.

The target wanted Kroger's P/L brand to deliver a happy and healthy experience. If Kroger could do that, their P/L brand would deliver Unique Advantage.

Kroger believed in the Brand Platform and developed an implementation plan. Elements of the plan included:

- Work with Kroger P/L suppliers to develop new products that were unique and fit the "happy and healthy" Unique Advantage, e.g., frozen pizza, yogurt, cereal. Some of the suppliers could make the transition to create value-added products. Some could not, i.e. their skill was low cost manufacturing, not innovation. Those suppliers had to be replaced. The product innovation process sought to develop "star" products in a few high visibility categories. The rationale: "star" products will help signal the intent of the new platform in a newsworthy way.
- Private Label was primarily executed in the center of the store where the "processed" products sit. The center of the store was increasingly becoming the dying part of the store as consumers sought the fresh product housed in the store's perimeter. All grocery stores sold fresh produce, but fresh produce was never included or marketed as a P/L offering. The Brand Platform needed to make fresh produce central.

A project was initiated to make that happen. Imagery was developed department by department to communicate a gold standard store experience, e.g., the bakery was to be reimagined as a French Bakery because the target believed that was the ultimate fresh bakery experience.

- Kroger Family Health Institute was designed to help families eat a healthier diet. The Brand Platform incorporated this asset into the execution plan. It had operated as a stand-alone service.
- Occasion Based Marketing was deployed to bring the Brand Platform to life in store For example, a promotion was developed "Eat. Laugh. Love" to bring together Kroger branded products into an easy to assemble family favorite meal.
- Design projects were undertaken to redesign the store experience beginning with the parking lot. Package design projects developed the overall look of the Kroger brand and how that look would work category by category.

The above process took more than a year to launch. Then the unexpected happened. The marketing person in charge of the project left the company. A few months later a replacement was hired whose career was exclusively in the grocery business. The former marketing person's experience was consumer packaged goods. The new person wanted to take a different approach to P/L not focused on an overarching Brand Platform but offering selected brands in selected categories each with its own brand name.

Lessons learned? The core value of the grocery industry is operations. Kroger had experimented with traditional marketing but, in the end, management was uncomfortable.

Susan's insights are telling. If the Brand Platform had been cloaked in "operations" terms it may have succeeded. "Culture eats strategy for breakfast."

Chapter 24

Irwin Gordon

Irwin Gordon. Formerly EVP Invitation Homes. SVP Global Branding PepsiCo.

Irwin began his career at Kellogg's Canada with responsibility for new product development. The Kellogg's name was an anathema to brand development as everything else was subsumed under the brand name. He also learned that the company did not have a defined brand building process.

Over time Irwin came to believe that the wellspring of branding is insight. Brand managers, however, are not good at insight…it's a different skill set. Insights are like fireflies…they can get lost in projects and company politics. It's the responsibility of the project leader to listen for and capture insight as it drives the conceptualization and execution of a brand building proposition.

It's critical and quite difficult to keep the insight alive through the brand building process. It's also key to have proof that the insight is valid and powerful. The more proof you have, the more momentum you give the project…though you may lose popularity along the way. With brand projects, everyone feels entitled to their opinion so with "proof" your insight is correct, you can move the conversation beyond opinion, i.e. a CEO who says, " I just don't believe it" or "I'll go with my gut."

You need to translate the insight into a concept form suitable for quantification which requires you to obtain the resources to make it happen.

The project leader cannot delegate participation in the branding process. The leader must attend the focus group with the internal and external brand team. Insights-driven people know that capturing insights is like capturing lightning in a bottle. You have to listen very carefully and when the "aha"

DOI: 10.4324/9781003223313-29

moment happens be able to communicate the insight to the team, so it's not lost.

Without an insight, messaging and design become beauty contests. The key is the story behind the design that explains the insight.

Why are brand people not insight people? Sometimes the answer is HR. HR's job descriptions capture the skills required in each job. If insight isn't in the description, it's not considered essential.

In today's world that can result in an overemphasis on brand analytics and AI.

In the best of all worlds, analytics and insight are both needed. Insight without analytics lacks proof. Analytics without insight equals "so what?" At a minimum, organizations should identify a few individuals with insight skills and reward them appropriately.

Another way to identify insight talent is to seek people who are creative problem solvers – good at divergent and convergent thinking and a talent to bring others along on the journey.

Case in point. Roger Enrico, PepsiCo's one of a kind creative problem solver and Irwin's boss.

Irwin believed that the Global Flat Chips project should be initiated. Roger agreed but also added: "And Irwin you are stupid enough to take it on."

Why stupid? Because the Frito Lay culture was operational in nature. The culture did not value insight. To win, you needed to uncover the insight, prove its validity, translate the insight in a way the organization understood so it could be effectively implemented and not lost or watered down along the way. The insight must become entrenched. And it's helpful if the CEO is insights driven and willing to mentor the project!

Global branding needs to establish design standards – both product design and graphic design.

At Frito Lay, the culture is operationally centered, brand agnostic and the organization is a loose federation of country managers. Without global standards, brand insight is easily lost or forgotten.

Before the Global Flat Chips Branding project was initiated, Marketplace P&L Studies were executed in each Frito Lay country. When the results were analyzed, it became clear that potato chips were the world's favorite snack.

The project vision... could the potato chips market operate like the cola market?

Could the Global Brand Platform make Lays the "cola of chips?"

The project insights suggested that could happen. Potato chip lovers (namely everyone) could not think of a simpler pleasure than potato chips. Their light taste and appearance explained why they were a simple pleasure, and the simple pleasures are what connects us all – and connection is the belief the target valued the most. And the simplest way to communicate simple pleasures is the kid in all of us – hence, the global power of the four little boys in the treehouse image.

And a focus group respondent in China called the winning package design "red silk wrapped around the sun" – the wrap, a circle icon, and the warm colors signify connection. And the lightness product attribute was the goal of R&D – to design the potato ship with the lightest taste.

Net, net, branding needs a process to identify the insight and prove its power, and partners within and outside the organization with an aptitude for creative problem solving. And creative problem-solving writ large – to ensure the Brand Platform is institutionalized – the well spring that is ever present.

Chapter 25

Dick Lochridge

Dick Lochridge. Former Board Member, Lowe's, PetSmart. Founder of Lochridge and Co, Partner at BCG, Marketing Manager at Norton Simon.

Dick's business philosophy was formed at the Boston Consulting Group. The management consulting firm focused on micro analysis... cost differences over time within and across companies and industries that could explain success or failure, e.g. the experience curve in manufacturing.

Dick's branding insights were derived from micro analysis, e.g., the revenue value and profitability of brands with higher customer loyalty, higher pricing, and lower costs over time.

Japanese studies and practices for process improvement gave Dick the tools to help organizations operate more efficiently...better able to market to their strengths and sustain success.

The process that Dick created merged customer market segmentations with operations. How to deliver customer's desired experience with better operational procedures. How to better organize against customer expectations.

An example of the process. A large makeup brand in Spain, the Revlon of Spain, was seen by consumers as the color authority. Consumers assumed that the brand would know the hot colors in lipstick each year. In fact, the company did not know. Dick's solution was to read sales of the large department stores that were the first to distribute this year's lipsticks and to instruct manufacturing to produce the bestselling varieties. The net effect, the brand maintained its color authority and optimized sales, never running out of stock. The behavioral data drove the organizational decisions.

DOI: 10.4324/9781003223313-30

Revlon, the color authority in the United States, wanted to enter the fragrance market. There were classic fragrances...Chanel 5, the most iconic... that had steady sales over decades. Revlon had no authority in fragrances. Their strategy was to target the young women who bought their lipsticks.

The brand Charlie was developed with a fresh scent with young appeal. Charlie's story was about a young woman asserting her will on the world... an aspirational story for a category that brands dreams. Charlie taps into universal values in a way similar to L'Oreal's message "I'm worth it." Both brands honor a woman's desire for an independent life...a different vision of herself...breaking society's perception of who she is.

Dick used micro economic data to strengthen service at Ford dealerships. Ford's process was to request all car owners requiring service to be at the dealership early in the morning. Car owners were asked for their service preference...the answer was that they wished to arrive at different times and, ideally, wanted to describe their car problem with the service technician who was going to fix it. The dealerships revamped their process to accommodate the consumer insight. The result...the car was fixed the first time every time. More importantly, Ford gained an advantage over Japanese car makers that translated into longer term loyalty.

Earlier in his career, Dick learned what doesn't work in brand building... seeking an advantage based on functional benefits. Ragu was the market leader in pasta sauce. Hunt's wanted to take them out. Hunt's developed and launched a recipe that was "extra thick and zesty" which was initially successful until Ragu developed their own version. Functional benefits can always be copied. Brands that endure have a story based on rich psychological insight that is extremely difficult to copy.

From an implementation standpoint, Dick's process requires that an organization lines up behind you. People fear change so you cannot assault the organization head on. What you can do is study the organization processes in minute detail to learn the bottlenecks. You can then change the process or procedure in a way that is not threatening and makes it easier to transition to a more efficient, customer facing organization.

In Dick's board of director role today, he says the downside of the data revolution. Mountains of data are now available that need to be analyzed... pounds of data with very little insight. The pendulum has now swung too far on the data side. The left brain, always the boss, is even more dominant. The left brain and right brain need to be in balance. Creative problem-solving needs both to win.

Chapter 26

Cindy Croatti

Cynthia Croatti. Executive VP UniFirst.

Cindy is the daughter of Aldo Croatti, who founded UniFirst in the 1930s. He effectively created the value proposition that established the industry, i.e., a industrial laundry rental service focused on uniforms worn by corporate employees. Prior to Aldo, industrial laundries washed clothes; the rental program…a five-year contract for laundry service…was the game changer.

Aldo had an unwavering focus on the customer and built the organization on highly responsive customer service. Aldo was succeeded by his son who was CEO for 20 years until his untimely death from a heart attack. His son's goal was to strengthen the sales organization as sales was the key to contract renewal and winning new contracts.

The good news…sales became a more asset. The bad news…the service reps who called on customers weekly over the five years of the contract… were not given the investment in training and technology to help them become more valuable to their customers.

Over a 20-year span, Cintas, founded around the same time as UniFirst, made two strategic investments: (1) expanding the product line to offer customers "one stop shopping" well beyond uniforms, and (2) acquiring and retaining employees with management leadership skills. The two investments enabled Cintas to become the dominant player.

Steve Sintros who was UniFirst CFO became CEO, the first non-family member to lead the business. Steve's mission is to build the management team that will enable UniFirst to compete effectively against a dominant competitor. One opportunity under development is branding. The uniform

DOI: 10.4324/9781003223313-31

services market is a commodity market. The overwhelming decision to renew a contract is price. Could UniFirst operate as a segmented player, focusing on uniforms, offering workers and their management a Brand Platform that justified premium pricing?

UniFirst's customers...the workers who wore their uniforms, and their management found the most meaning in their personal and professional relationships. Their families, their customers, and their co-workers depend on them. They take great pride supporting those that depend on them.

The desired experience they seek is to feel "unstoppable"...a feeling that inspires them to be at the top of their game...inspires them to succeed.

UniFirst's Unique Advantage is its commitment to always be there for their customers.

To UniFirst service reps, it's all about the customer...their relationships are like good friends. It's a service benefit UniFirst can deliver, given its core family culture that created the brand and is still the North Star.

UnIFirst is now in the process of building the leadership skills to deliver the Brand Platform at scale. Strategic planning and leadership training will ensure the internal organization internalizes the Platform and is inspired to deliver it.

Chapter 27

Bruce Bader

Bruce Bader. Retired Research Fellow Procter & Gamble.

For Bruce, success is a willingness to get out of the box. P&G is a large, complex, bureaucratic organization that runs on numbers. Success is the result of an individual developing an idea and having the courage to drive the idea through the system. It's also important to have coverage from a senior manager. Lewis and Clark were the explorers on the ground and their sponsors resided in the federal government.

Our Pampers project is a good example of Bruce's guiding principles. P&G never went to "outside resources" for help solving problems. Bruce believed he needed to do so because P&G had been unsuccessful reviving Pampers. The Brand's revenue had been flat for more than a decade…unacceptable performance for one of the three brands that drove the company's stock price.

Bruce's mentors gave him the freedom to attack the problem his way. Their only advice was that the process be executed in Japan where the General Manager, Hiroko Wada, was the first woman GM at any Japanese company. Wada San supported the project which required her people to work 16 days…8 hours on their day job, 8 hours on the Pampers project. The project would have encountered deep skepticism in the much more bureaucratic US company.

Bruce had excellent success applying consumer modeling to revive the Pantene business. He viewed our process as another approach to consumer or human modeling.

The Cone of Learning was in many ways the template that guided his management of innovation projects like Pampers. The Cone of Learning

DOI: 10.4324/9781003223313-32

Pyramid states that we retain 5% of a lecture, 10% of what we read, 20% of audio visual, 30% of demonstration, 50% from discussion, 75% practice doing, 90% when we teach others.

The project leader is the Magician Archetype who never tells people what to do but exposes them to insights and ideas which they can choose or not choose to adopt.

It's critical to involve people in the process...ideally a cross-functional and cross-cultural team.

The team attends all the research sessions...the moment of truth is seeing the consumer's eyes light up. It's at that moment the team realizes...feels... the power of insight or idea to do something meaningful for the consumer.

Once the team sees the truth that will create brand magic, the hard work begins...how to persuade the bureaucracy to buy in. It's necessary to make the whole experience visible to the organization.

It's also necessary to have the right ways to measure your innovation. P&G's traditional measures were focused on physical product features and functions. If that's what you measure, you are guaranteed to make incremental improvements at best. To have a breakthrough, you need a way to measure a breakthrough. The solution was to measure consumer ideals. Against ideals, a good idea may score 20% or 30% out of 100%. But you now have the right scale and better way to measure.

Metaphors are good ways to make it real for the organization. If a diaper is being designed for a new-born baby, a commode is an excellent metaphor. It inspires designers to create a product that is "different in kind"... light years away from incrementalism.

Bruce's academic training was in science...chemistry. Consumer modeling is hard, if not impossible to capture via the scientific method. It's a different kind of knowledge...about the feelings that drive our behavior, create meaning in our lives. Bruce has met a number of highly successful scientists... technically at the top of their game who become photographers as a way to uncover emotional truths...who wanted to go beyond the game they know.

Within organizations like P&G, you need to identify the right kind of people to be involved...they will be guides for the team. And they need to be fearless to fight the status quo.

He sees an opportunity to create two types of career paths: (1) managers who operate within well-defined formulas and systems with the end goal to improve productivity and sales(2) leaders whose role is visionary, helping others discover the emotional truths and creative processes that lead to innovation breakthroughs.

Stated another way, companies need to have a performance culture that delivers sales results and a learning culture that is not responsible for sales but is charged with the responsibility for big, step change innovation. Many of P&G's big breakthroughs took decades to develop. Bruce spent the last part of his career helping P&G teams around the world how to interact with consumers in a way that leads to big ideas…1–2 people can make a difference.

In many ways, Bruce's career helps P&G move beyond the cultural belief that "we are the experts" to embrace the idea that useful knowledge is available outside the company. P&G needs to understand and apply that insight so the culture evolves, reflecting new truths that will drive future success.

A few last thoughts. Bruce's experience with my process mirrors my own: the process can be applied to any problem…organizational development, societal challenges, education reform.

Enlightened leadership will take us on the journey of discovery and universal human truths will be our compass.

Chapter 28

Jesper Nordengaard

Jesper Nordengaard. CEO Hill's Pet Products.

Branding is about knowing who you are...knowing what role your brand plays in people's lives.

In Hill's case, the brand is about the science of pet food...Hill's from inception is about a deep understanding of pet biology and plant biology... applying that knowledge to create products that maintain and improve the pet's health. Hill's product formulations follow their function in the pet's body.

The founder of Hill's had that vision. Each new generation of managers needs to share and live that vision.

And marketers must be super disciplined about innovation and branding initiatives to be sure the brand does not go off track...chasing the next shiny thing vs the science-based charter.

One test is to ask yourself if your brand were to stop existing, what would consumers miss? If you know who you are and the value you play in people's lives is clear, you have a strong brand story that promotes loyalty.

Historically Hill's has been a strong product organization but a less strong brand organization.

A strong brand organization is clear about what it is and what it is not. Freeze-dried pet food, raw pet food does not fit the Hill's science-based story.

Marketers must understand that Hill's needs deep insight into its target audience to win over the long term. Marketers also needs to know that some consumers will reject the brand and that's OK. The Hill's story is not for them. To attempt to be all things to all people is a recipe for disaster.

DOI: 10.4324/9781003223313-33

Senior leadership needs to train the organization to be tolerant of different business styles, e.g., digital marketers are needed to help Hill's optimize online distribution which is expected to control 50% of pet food sales in a few years.

To operate in an ever-changing environment, the concepts of the digital world need to bridge to the traditional marketing world. It's not one or the other. For many years, Colgate has attracted talent that wants to stay with the company for a lifetime. Some employees needed today may not share that philosophy.

Jesper believes the eight years his eight years at Hill's has been highly instructive. It's given him the time to internalize the brand's DNA...to manage through difficult times and good times...to learn how to incorporate new initiatives that may take time (sometimes we give up too fast on things).

He thinks the company would benefit from a Chief Experience Officer...a person dedicated to ensuring each of the many ways a consumer encounters the brand is optimal. If the experience is consistently positive, the opportunity for loyalty is enhanced.

Chapter 29

Chris Sinclair

Chris Sinclair. CEO at Mattel, President at PepsiCo International. Marketing Manager at General Foods (now Kraft).

Entry level positions at brand building organizations and marketing focused undergraduate and graduate schools, give employees a marketing foundation. Marketing training beyond the basics does not exist. The lessons about brand-building are self-taught.

In Chris's case, he learned the value of developing benefits that resonated with consumers on a much deeper level.

As one example, the best of the best images from a Brand Platform helped his organization

"feel" the consumer truths as well as the stories they told about why the winning images meant so much to them...connected to beliefs they lived by.

On a related note, R&D folks at P&G had images from our Brand Platform at their workstations. When I asked why, they said the images inspired them to design product against the experience the image suggested. From R&D's perspective, the tacit knowledge captured in an image was a superior way to present a product development brief.

To successfully implement a Brand Platform requires execution at all consumer touch points. The Global Flat Chips Brand Platform was executed:

- in product: R&D reformulated Lays to be the lightest potato chip...the consumer gold standard.
- in package design: to communicate Harmony...the potato chips are harmony metaphor that expressed the target's Fundamental Belief.
- in global advertising: copy (ads with images and music and no words) captured the "kid in all of us" feeling that connects us all.

DOI: 10.4324/9781003223313-34

Another PepsiCo Brand successfully applied the Brand Platform Success Model...Pepsi Max.

To set the stage, Diet Pepsi was the vehicle driving total Pepsi growth in Europe. Diet Pepsi was consumed primarily by females and its sales were starting to slow as the segment became saturated.

The decision was made to develop a new low/no calorie cola targeted to young/teen males.

Young males, heavy cola consumers, rejected Diet Pepsi as too "girly".

The young males selected images depicting the dark, mysterious taste of cola...imagery quite the opposite of the more "clinical" imagery of diet colas.

R&D created a Pepsi Max formulation with the mouth feel and rich taste of regular cola.

The Pepsi Max tagline: Max the Taste. Axe the Sugar. The Brand was a smashing success. The Brand signaled the masculine credentials and real cola experience the boys wanted.

Chris's bottom line: success implementing a Brand Platform is a function of senior management leading the charge to bring the Platform to life.

Chapter 30

Jim Koch

Jim Koch, Founder of the Boston Beer Company.

Jim created Sam Adams Boston Lager, the success of which helped him create the craft beer movement. Sam Adams was chosen as the brand name because Sam Adams was a brewer of rich, flavorful beers as well as a patriot who fought to support the American Revolution. And Jim wanted to revolutionize the American beer industry.

Jim's great grandfather created a lager beer in his native Germany. Jim thought the recipe might create a flavorful beer experience that would be new and interesting to the American beer palate.

In retrospect, creating Boston Lager was the easy part. The hard part was selling it...convincing bar owners to distribute it and beer drinkers to drink it.

Jim's wish is that Sam Adams branding would emerge fully formed like Minerva from Zeus' head. The reality was that the Boston Beer process was trial and error, continuous learning, slowly becoming a brand.

Jim's first business card stated: "America's Only Classic Lager"...a sharp contrast with the mass produced, mass marketed American beers. But telling people Sam Adams is Classic Lager is an assertion...like going into a cocktail party telling everyone you are a quality person. Who cares? And what does it mean anyway?

The real work was painstaking...going to bars, doing promotions, night after night. One on ones with real beer drinkers. What do you consider quality beer? The imports. Did you know they are mass produced like the big American beer brands? Would you be willing to try Sam Adams? If you don't like it, I'll buy you the import of your choice.

DOI: 10.4324/9781003223313-35

The above process was practiced night after night. Jim and his sales team were listening carefully to every beer drinker and exploring concepts to explain what Sam Adams was all about. Jim and team cracked the code with the words "handcrafted in small batches." That collection of words explained why Sam Adams was high quality and unique vs the mass-produced beers. That code helped create the Sam Adams brand and the craft beer category.

Early on, Jim bartered beer for air-time with local radio stations. The stations asked Jim what time slots he wanted. He learned that the cheapest airtime was 1–2 am. Jim said that's the time he wanted…when bartenders and servers were going home from work.

Jim did a couple of other things that other craft brewers did not do. He created a sales force to continue the nightly work of building a brand, one drinker at a time. His competitors loved brewing beer which is admittedly a lot of fun, but they failed to do the hard work of winning over new drinkers. Ultimately no beer drinker is loyal to one beer. The key is to become part of the beer drinkers brand set and that creates the annuity.

From the standpoint of first principles, Sam Adams proved that changes in behavior produce changes in attitude. Many beer drinkers tried Sam Adams and a good percentage found they really liked a more flavorful beer.

For them, the mass-produced beer tasted watered down. They preferred the richer taste. Many other beer drinkers found Sam was too strong vs what they were used to. So, Sam was built among the beer drinkers who enjoyed a richer beer experience.

I became involved with Jim years after he had launched Sam Adams. The brand had grown steadily over those years sourcing its volume primarily from imported beers. At about the 15-year mark sales had flattened. Jim's analysis was that Sam Adams growth was in large part trial, i.e., many (mass market) beer drinkers tried the brand but did not commit to regular usage… their taste buds found the beer too strong.

Jim sought a Brand Platform that would reignite sales growth. The Fundamental Belief was Authenticity. Beer drinkers wanted to live an authentic life. No games, no pretenses. They wanted fulfilling careers. They wanted relationships that were real and never phony. Sam Adams and Jim were a metaphor that linked to their Beliefs. The Brand had the authentic taste of an American original. Jim had pursued his dreams to create Boston Beer. The marketing and advertising brought the Platform to life and sales rebounded.

Sam Adams is a good demonstration of creating a category by creating a brand. Twisted Tea, Angry Orchard, and most recently, Truly are other examples. Boston Beer's portfolio is built on identifying product concepts that offer a fresh taste experience and via branding become successful category builders.

Looking to the future, Jim feels the company must keep up with its consumers. Consumers are changing in their attitudes toward life, about products and companies they admire and support, about their consumption of media. Boston Beer people must continue their commitment to lifelong learning.

Chapter 31

Dan Dillon

Dan Dillon. CEO ASU Enterprise Partners. Formerly, CMO of ASU, Marketing Management at Coca Cola and HJ Heinz.

Dan's branding philosophy is the same as mine. The Brand Platform is the first and most important step. The Platform drives every decision.

The Brand Platform aligns everyone and, in so doing, avoids people from having different interpretations of the strategy. Marketing is one of the few disciplines where everyone has an opinion…finance, operations, engineering all have ideas about how a brand should be marketed.

Dan believes that branding should be data driven and not a popularity contest. Everyone's point of view is welcome but data rules. If the new advertising has scored well with the target audience, that's the direction the brand should take.

When things do not go as planned, companies sometimes get off track chasing the latest and greatest features and functions. On other occasions validation research is not conducted.

The lesson to be learned is to trust the Brand Platform. It was built from deep insight into target customers…what they wish for and how the brand will serve them. Research validated the Platform. It's the North Star. Follow the North Star and your odds of winning go way up.

DOI: 10.4324/9781003223313-36

Chapter 32

Alan Ives

Alan Ives. Executive Creative Director ABC News.

For Alan, branding is a political campaign. The object is to win votes. In the case of television, you need to win viewers' votes every day. The secret to brand messaging is to know what's in viewers' hearts and how to tell a news story that touches their feelings. Two master non-fiction storytellers that Alan greatly admires are Barbara Walters and Diane Sawyer. They personified his branding philosophy. Both women had a clear sense of who they were. Both understood the story was not about them. What mattered was why the story mattered...why it was a story worth telling. And to never talk at the viewer but with the viewer.

The attitudes and persona of the two women were in sharp contrast to conventional journalism. The assumption was that the journalist knew what was important and his job was to educate the viewer, i.e., the viewer needs to learn to eat broccoli. Empathy and heartfelt were not in the equation.

Alan and I were part of the team who worked with Ben Sherwood when he was brought in as the ABC News President. At that time, ABC News was a highly demoralized organization...many people had been let go, linear TV news was not growing, and ABC News was not a ratings leader. Ben was a lightning rod of change. He instilled passion and a sense of purpose to the organization.

Our branding project was one of the initiatives Ben used to revitalize the organization. The project was designed to teach the organization what news viewers sought from news and what ABC News should do to meet their news needs and aspirations. News viewers wanted a big picture understanding of their world so they could make better life decisions.

DOI: 10.4324/9781003223313-37

The ABC News properties included GMA, World News Tonight, and This Week. The talent on those shows brought the brand story to life. Viewers find Robin Roberts, George Stephanopoulos, Michael Strahan, and David Muir to be approachable and trustworthy...the foundation attributes of a news brand. Robin feels warm and George feels brainy...but both are approachable in their own way. David Muir is a great example of personal branding. To David, every detail matters. When he tells the story of Syrian children he is one on one at the border with the kids. He knows what he wants the viewer to take away from that story, i.e., feeling what those kids are experiencing. The feeling is the way the news story gets to the heart of things. My process is about the brand feeling overall. David's storytelling is about one specific event. The key is that that brand is brought to life by every ABC News journalist in every story every day.

The impact of heartfelt storytelling across ABC News properties is a revitalized brand with ratings leadership over the past decade.

Chapter 33

Gary Matthews

Gary Matthews. CEO Seven Oaks Acquisition Corporation. Formerly, Private Equity Managing Director, Morgan Stanley, Managing Director, Guinness.

Gary values branding for its ability to increase margins and secure premium pricing. He ran Guinness in the United States. When he inherited the Brand, Guinness had two unique equities: a differentiated product...a bitter tasting stout with a creamy head...and an Irish heritage. The issue going forward was how to drive the Brand's growth...after years of flat sales.

A three part strategy was developed: (1) develop the essence of the Brand; (2) increase marketing spend, importantly, above the line media... Guinness had never run TV advertising...a Win Your Own Pub in Ireland was an effective promotion that leveraged the Irish heritage; and (3) new product innovation...Guinness in a can that contained a widget that released nitrogen that mimicked the Guinness classic pour and creamy finish.

The three-part strategy ignited Guinness growth. Guinness was only distributed on premises in Irish pubs and bars catering to beer drinkers who are willing and able to pay premium prices for premium products. The advertising and promotion jump started Guinness growth in its traditional bar channel. The new Guinness in a can product opened up the off-premise channel for the first time. Off premise channels such as supermarkets control about 75% of beer volume. The on-premise bars are where beers are sampled. Guinness was now attracting new beer drinkers in bars who, in turn, could now for the first time find the Brand at the supermarket and experience the brand at home or take to a party.

DOI: 10.4324/9781003223313-38

Guinness' Irish heritage links well to the beer drinkers' Desired Experience...the joy, the humor, the good will of Irish culture. The heritage is meaningful to beer drinkers broadly...not just those of Irish descent.

On a management level, Gary feels that most marketing teams are highly skilled left-brain thinkers. Skills that are needed for all the analysis required for marketing programs, e.g., volume by segment, ROI. What's more problematic is analysis of the power of emotional benefits. The challenge for senior management is to translate the Brand Platform in a way the organization can understand and implement it. From my experience, as a first step, a company's culture needs to be made explicit in order to understand the best way to manage the implementation of a new Brand Platform...importantly, the emotional elements of the Platform.

Chapter 34

Tony Magee

Tony Magee. Founder of Lagunitas Brewing Company.

Tony's insights should be understood within the context of a company founder. My interviews include two founders, Tony and Jim Koch. The passion of the founders' contrasts with corporate executives who manage a business but did not create it.

For Tony, branding begins with authenticity. He's concerned the word authenticity is used so often it almost loses its meaning. Tony focuses on the "auth" root of authenticity…the author of the exposition. The author of a brand must be somebody who has something to say.

He must "own" the brand and not "ape" someone else.

The second word is storytelling…another word so overused in branding to be close to BS.

Storytelling to Tony means the brand author knows what story he wants to tell and why he wants to tell it.

The Hero's Journey offers a path for brand building. The Hero must accept the Call to Adventure…the invitation to author an original story that can with success transform the author and all of us. It's Tony's way to teach the true meaning of authentic brand building. Brand building is the Hero's Journey.

He cites a few great brand builders including Henry Ford. Ford built a brand that matters…endures over time. No one ever did what Henry Ford did. Ford has become part of the American terra firma. The Beatles is another brand that matters…authentic with a unique story to tell. So is Paul Newman. When you hear about Newman's Own brand the Newman brand is front and center in our consciousness.

DOI: 10.4324/9781003223313-39

Tony authored the Lagunitas story. The brand owns a welcoming spirit reflecting its beer and a feeling of inclusiveness experienced by everyone. After establishing leadership of the IPA category in the US, Tony partnered with Heineken to expand the Brand globally.

Tony's vision was that the spirit of freedom, adventure, and rejuvenation reflected in the Brand could ultimately inform and expand the Heineken corporate culture. It did not.

Heineken became a global giant by putting in place the structure and systems that can manage a vast cast of employees and assets. The entrepreneurial seed of Lagunitas brand cannot be planted in a culture that punishes failure. The Lagunitas acquisition by Heineken became a Harvard Business School case exploring the benefits and barriers of large, complex corporations buying and integrating highly successful brands...mostly, not a good track record.

CONSULTANT
INTERVIEWS

Chapter 35

What Can My Consultants Teach Us?

What can my consultants teach us about the brand building process?

What they all shared was a strong desire to learn about branding. To succeed at my company, they all needed to believe in and commit to the brand building process. In the beginning, we thought that consultants should have a balanced intellect...capable of strategic thinking and intuitive creativity. The process needed both sets of skills as a project moved between divergent and convergent thinking. One other shared quality. Our consultants were at the entry point of their careers...either just out of college or a few years post college. Nonetheless, their position demanded that they express their beliefs and ideas. The brand building process is a collaboration. Everyone's ideas matter and contribute to the ultimate solution. If someone was afraid to speak up, they had to conquer that fear. We'd help them but they must decide to make that happen. I'm reminded of the famous tagline from the Shawshank Redemption: "Fear keeps us prisoner. Hope sets us free."

Highly successful consultants exhibited a wide range of talents. To give you a flavor ...

- an actress looking to change career directions. Her acting motto served her well: "Acting is reacting." Not too much of a leap from consumer insight into brand proposition,
- a brand manager, trained in rigorous analysis, succeeded because she was more thorough...no stone left unturned,

DOI: 10.4324/9781003223313-41

- a natural leader, not as skilled at creative development as her peers, but gifted in helping everyone including herself, meets the goals of a project,
- a creative talent, superb at generative thinking, less so with convergent thinking, marketed to her strength while backfilling her ability at the analysis,
- a philosophy major seeking to define the first principles of brand building,
- talent trained at ad agencies seeking a strategic foundation for branding,
- a designer...integrating the power of design with brand strategy.

Chapter 36

Milo Rodriguez

Milo Rodriguez. Strategic Advisor to Kosterina, Senior Associate, Barclays, Senior Consultant, Lubin Lawrence.

Milo majored in psychology and art history in college. She was looking for a way to apply her academic interests. Marketing seemed a good way to bridge psychology with business.

She had an on-going perception that the best brands had a deep understanding of their consumers. Her example is Ralph Lauren. Milo's dad was an immigrant from Nicaragua. To her dad, Ralph Lauren, the man himself and his clothing, were the American Dream. From a very young age, Milo felt the power of a Brand to inspire and build an enduring emotional connection.

Milo joined LLI right out of college. Initially, she focused on the mechanics of the process. Her conversations with other consultants helped craft the stimuli and design the research.

The focus groups with customers cracked the code on the process. When she was leading a group, respondents would often give her their "knee jerk" or superficial answers to her questions. She would then use visual and verbal stimuli to unlock deeper insight...what the brand said about the consumer...how it spoke to them. She spoke to consumers all over the world, virtually all of whom were very different from her...from first-time moms to construction workers. She needed to be friendly and open and to never lead them. She needed to create an environment that made them comfortable sharing their fears, hopes, and dreams, fundamental beliefs.

The process worked best when the client had strong beliefs about their brand and the power of branding. Disney is a classic example. Disney

DOI: 10.4324/9781003223313-42

people know they are in the "hit" business and innovation is key to success. They are skilled at translating consumer insights and Brand Platforms into effective branding programs.

The process was less successful in corporations with highly political cultures...where "going along to get along" ruled the day. The appetite for risk was virtually non-existent. However, even in that type of environment, translating the consumer truths into tangible brand elements such as product, package design, could help make the Brand Platform pay off.

On a larger scale, most corporate people are valued for their analytical capability. To people with a decided analytical mindset, consumer feelings are "fluff." To counter "fluff," management must demonstrate why, for example, Tide has led the detergent category for 70 years at a premium price while detergent brand formulations are quite similar. Proof that great branding really pays off.

Chapter 37

Shira Machleder

Shira Machleder. Senior Marketing Manager at Amazon, Marketing Director at American Express, Senior Consultant at Lubin Lawrence.

Shira studied psychology and sociology in college. She felt marketing was a logical fit with her academic interests, i.e., how people interact with brands. Lubin Lawrence integrated art and science...bridged the gap between the right brain and the left brain...looking for the connections between data and emotions and translating the insight into messaging. The branding framework applies to many kinds of businesses...a framework many clients were not considering.

For Shira, listening to the consumer was key. Visual and verbal stimuli helped the consumer teach us the values they lived by and feelings that expressed their aspirations in life and the brand benefits that link to those aspirations.

The iterative nature of the process helped consumers express brand building ideas.

Shira also believes the process works best when applied to macro branding issues where the project output guides product innovation, design, and messaging. The process is not as impactful on smaller issues like flanker brand development.

A key success driver is starting the process with consumers' fundamental values and beliefs.

DOI: 10.4324/9781003223313-43

Chapter 38

Mike Lubin

Mike Lubin. Vice President-Growth at Babylon, Managing Director at Sterling Rice, Senior Consultant at Lubin Lawrence.

Mike was a philosophy major in college. He was interested in learning how to solve complex problems. Lubin Lawrence was appealing because brand building is a complex problem that needed a strategic solution.

Mike believes the process at its core is a way to develop a fundamental understanding of human beings. Most people in business do not know how to develop that understanding, nor how to harness that insight to drive strategy. People, whether they realize it or not, have blinders on...or lack the glasses to see these truths.

Today, many companies are technology driven. Product first. The focus is how to sell the product. This approach could benefit from understanding the mind of the market...the wider context within which your product sits...and how to communicate with your customers in a more meaningful way.

The process works when leaders are believers...they may or may not have any marketing training, but what they share is an intuitive belief that the process will pay big dividends.

If they are believers, they will give the process the time it needs. And not be a slave to the timeline driver.

In Mike's current role, he manages the sales organization. He insists that his sales team understand and codify the fundamental beliefs of their prospects first before they attempt to sell anything. Invariably, salespeople gain insight they didn't expect...truths they never knew...that helps them reframe their approach and better manage the relationship. Mike has built metrics to measure how well the sales team understands the fundamental beliefs of prospects. And in business: "you get what you measure."

DOI: 10.4324/9781003223313-44

Chapter 39

Sheri Harris

Sheri Harris. Strategy Director at Nimbly. Senior Consultant at Lubin Lawrence.

Sheri studied semiotics…how signs and symbols…visual and linguistic… create meaning in our lives. Her academic training gave her a unique lens to understand and apply my process.

She has worked in branding her entire career.

I asked Sheri where branding is today and how it got there. She sees branding now as more personal, reflecting the data-driven explosion in recent years. One-on-one branding, given how much is known about an individual's behavior. Each person is a data point.

Another factor…millennials or younger consumers broadly believe branding is not authentic. As a result, marketers seek to appeal to cultural trends, e.g. diversity, LGBTQ, inclusion. Their messaging is often not an authentic portrait, e.g., an Asian family in a typically "white picket fence" setting. Reality is not portrayed. The messaging is opportunistic, not genuine.

Branding should be based upon universal emotional truths…both consumer truths and the truths behind a company's purpose…not pandering.

Markets and cultural "semiotics" are moving at a rapid pace. Even emojis are showing their generational age. The emoji communicating I'm laughing so hard I'm crying belongs to people over 25. Under 25 skull and crossbones says I died laughing. Tik Tok is moving us along at a record speed.

Within corporations, younger marketers skew social media; older marketers, traditional ads.

And data drives the analysis…to the point of data overload. Virtually no insight from stories.

DOI: 10.4324/9781003223313-45

We seem to have two languages of marketing with data language in the driver's seat.

What should be done to improve branding effectiveness in the future? From the perspective of large, complex organizations, there is a need for "agility." It takes two years to do anything – internal silos, risk aversion are among the barriers. Culture eats strategy for breakfast and the big company culture is risk averse. Some big companies fight the tendency with innovation centers... "garages" ...that innovate quickly. And their success in the marketplace can be copied quickly, at scale, by the broader organization.

We all watch disruptors, usually small operations, push the envelope to make big ideas happen...which the big operators quickly copy. Bud Light Seltzer is a good example. Bud Light has scale, but their offering is "me too" and smaller competitors who invented the category...White Claw and Truly... maintain category leadership.

Brands like Toms had a social purpose driven from the outset. Now it's the price of entry for all brands.

For Sheri, the moments of truth that matter reflect on her academic training in semiotics and are reinforced in the process...the patterns of truth from imagery, music, and language.

Universal truths underpin the strongest Brand Platforms – the Platforms that become a Brand's North Star.

And if a company has a North Star Platform, what separates the winners from the losers in the marketplace? Translation and activation.

The brand team needs to know that the Brand Platform is not the Campaign Platform. They must manage the translation process to be sure that effective messaging and design are created and implemented. The truth of the Platform must be decoded.

And how does Sheri teach entry point marketers about universal truths? She has them do research to go beyond what consumers say is the truth to why it's important. Not "what" but "so what?"...the underlying emotional truths that underpin great branding.

Chapter 40

Rose Lee

Rose Lee. Managing Director Credit Suisse, Formerly Managing Director, Goldman Sachs. Senior Consultant Lubin Lawrence.

What drives business success? (1) A clear vision and strategy in place... well-articulated to internal and external stakeholders; (2) Good leaders to execute the vision...process leaders and strategy leaders; (3) Customer loyalty based on "we will always be there for you" customer service.

Rose's team develops custom trading products for its customers. The products are complex, better than competitive products, ...a unique new category of product. The products deliver upside and downside risk/rewards based on each client's requirements.

To create custom products, Rose needs to have a deep understanding of each customer...his or her values, investment goals, and risk tolerance. The understanding guides product development and the sales approach to educate the clients about how the product works.

Rose uses the process to frame and focus product development. She develops insight into each element of the Brand Platform...the client's fundamental human beliefs, their desired professional experience, the new product's unique advantage, and the benefits that support the unique advantage.

Two core beliefs underpin Rose's approach to business. She has a business owner's mindset...how a company does is a reflection of her and her team. She thinks like an entrepreneur...always seeking to do more, do better, stretch your wings. She inherited her beliefs from her parents who emigrated to the US from Korea when she was very young. They wanted a better life for Rose, and her brother. They knew hardly any English and had to start from the bottom of the economic ladder.

When we worked together, Rose was a leader, not a manager. Her leadership qualities made me and the people who worked for her better.

Chapter 41

Kristin Veley

Kristin Veley. Brand Management Diageo. Research Director Boston Beer. Senior Consultant Lubin Lawrence.

What drives project success?

(1) Ask big picture questions. Who is the target? What are their most important beliefs? What are their hopes and dreams? What is this brand all about? What is the company all about that markets this brand? Big picture questions beget big picture answers.

Ask small questions and you get small solutions.

(2) Picture power. All the information we need to understand the world comes from our senses...all knowledge is embodied. And our sense of sight is uniquely powerful...human thought is imaged based. And just for good measure...one picture is worth a thousand words.

When consumers select a few images from hundreds, we should listen carefully. The few images were selected because they tie to important consumer values. Strategy is almost exclusively expressed in words. And that is unfortunate because strategy excludes the insight into tacit knowledge that imagery is uniquely capable of providing. And once an image is selected, the consumer is able to tell a story that explains the meaning behind the image...insight that can crack the code on a branding challenge.

As an example, focus group respondents were asked to draw an image that explained the essence of Hunt's tomato products. One respondent drew an image of a fresh tomato. We asked why a fresh tomato when Hunt's products are all canned? Her answer: Hunt's equals a fresh tomato. In her mind, Hunt's wasn't a canned product and that's why she was loyal.

DOI: 10.4324/9781003223313-47

(3) Respect history. There is a tendency when a new marketing team takes over a brand, they want to put their own stamp on it...often wanting to redo everything. Core brand values should stand the test of time. Make big changes only after you have reviewed the history and decided everything needs to be tossed out.

Case in point. MasterCard was the mainstream leader of the mass credit card market with the tagline: "So Worldly. So Welcome." The message: the card is accepted everywhere, and the card holder is esteemed as a worldly person. The new marketing team decided they didn't like the positioning, so they tossed it out. The Visa team, better students of history, created advertising within weeks...Visa. Everywhere you want to be...that enabled them to gain and sustain global category leadership. Visa applied MasterCard's insight which MasterCard had chosen to ignore.

There was a time when a few brand-driven companies knew the power of their brand and decided to protect the brand with an executive who was deemed the keeper of the brand keys.

Such a role doesn't fit easily into an organization chart and top management has to offer cover for the executive for him or her to be effective.

(4) Think team journey. Cross-functional teams supported by senior management are the best way to go on the brand building journey. It's highly collaborative. And the moment of truth is often just after a focus group is completed and the team meets to discuss the learning. The relevant data is shared, and the conversation aligns on the critical insight that will drive the branding. Everyone is encouraged to speak up. Team members learn from each other. The team is in a much better position to explain the insight to people who were unable to attend the focus group.

(5) Brand building is creative work. A company needs to hire and promote people skilled with the talent to uncover insights and translate into brand concepts. The perfect combo is creative talent and analytical talent working together.

IMPLEMENTATION TECHNIQUES AND TACTICS

Chapter 42

Focus Group Research

Focus groups are best used to gather deep insight into the issues that impact the branding process. They are exploratory in nature and not really designed to evaluate ideas. Evaluation is usually about quantitative research.

Focus groups are often given a bad rap by marketing experts and academics for a few reasons:

- the leader effect. Assume a focus group of 5–10 respondents. If one or two respondents are highly vocal and with strong opinions, they will dominate the discussion. Less aggressive respondents will either go along to get along or just not offer their thinking. Net, net, questions arise about the validity of the focus group output.
- respondents have sharply different values and ideas. The focus group becomes a boxing match of sharply different viewpoints but not clear insight on the issues that prompted the research in the first place.

Given the above, why do we use focus groups or dyads or one-on-one interviews to generate insights and brand hypotheses? Simply put, because we have developed a focus group process that overcomes the above objections. Here's how:

- Recruiting Focus Group Respondents. The guiding principle is homogeneity. Respondents in each focus group should share similar values, attitudes, and behaviors. As an example, if we wish to study male teens who love colas, they should all be 17 years old and juniors in high

DOI: 10.4324/9781003223313-49

school, i.e. share a common life stage. The result is the absence of controversy and, more to the point, the group learns early on, they share common views which usually builds bonds and collaboration.

■ Focus Group Pre-work. Respondents fill out benefit forms privately before the group begins. The step avoids leader bias because each respondent has voted on the benefits that personally motivate him or her prior to group discussion.

■ Focus Group Exercises. The focus group typically required homework, e.g., respondents are asked to find 4–5 images that teach us who you are...select 4–5 images that communicate the brand essence of Coca Cola. The homework, like the pre-work benefit selection, is done privately and by definition, not influenced by other respondents. The respondents are exposed to verbal and visual stimuli which impact our mind in different ways. The research is analyzed for patterns of truth across the exercises which increases the odds of an unbiased truth.

All knowledge is embodied. Humans receive information through our senses. The research is designed to make that knowledge explicit so we can build our hypotheses. That's why we use visual stimuli...human knowledge is image-based...to extract embodied insight. We also on occasion use musical stimuli because music taps into entirely different parts of the brain. We've also used sensory stimuli because our sense of smell is another way, we gather knowledge.

A quick note on musical stimuli. We've learned that music stimuli must be instrumental only. Lyrics affect us in a different way. We don't want to make the stimuli too complex, hence, instrumental only.

We also learned the instrumental music must be unrecognizable, i.e., not a hit song the respondents might recognize. If they know the music, it may have a particular memory attached which impedes learning, e.g. That's my sister's favorite song and I hate it.

We play 4–6 instrumental pieces of music. After each selection, we ask respondents to write down the words that express how the music made them feel...and which musical selection best fits with their favorite brand hypothesis and why. The goal with music and imagery is to learn which "feeling" was most aspirational...suggesting the kind of experience they are wishing for.

Net, net, we take a number of steps when we conduct qualitative research to overcome barriers to the truth. Statisticians describe our approach as "quali-quant" because of our in-depth screening/recruiting process. They believe our small sample of respondents are projectable, given the "homogeneity" of our screener.

There is another less tangible factor that contributes to the power of the insights...we ask respondents to teach us about their Fundamental Human Beliefs and Desired Experiences. Respondents are rarely asked to tell the story about their most important beliefs and hopes and dreams. It's our observation that respondents value the opportunity to share their story which usually reveals the common bonds shared by the group. As a result, respondents take their mission to build their ideal brand seriously as it's tied to the beliefs and aspirations that give their life meaning.

Chapter 43

The Power of Imagery to Inform Brand Platform Development

Visuals have been far and away the most valuable research stimuli. Human thought is imaged based. We have uncovered a few images that give us amazingly rich insight into the hearts and minds of consumers. Weight Watcher members selected an image of a woman wearing a size 12 or 14 suit admiring her image reflected in a store window. The smile on her face said she was pleased by her appearance...that she had high self-esteem. It was the perfect image for the Weight Watcher Brand Platform.

The Desired Experience of Weight Watcher members and prospective members is to feel a high sense of self-esteem. Teaching members how to take charge of their food intake so they could lose weight is the functional benefit of the brand. But the ultimate benefit is emotional...to feel better about oneself...to have a positive outlook.

Another near perfect image is a mom wearing her graduation gown at her college graduation. She has a big smile on her face and is holding her young son in her arms. He is wearing her graduation cap. The image was selected by all prospects considering going to school online to earn their college degree. The core target audience for an online degree is in the workforce with an average age of 33. Many are married with children. The decision to go back to school is daunting financially and emotionally. The rewards are mighty including a new career path with substantial upward mobility. The image is victory...the feeling of hard-earned accomplishment.

DOI: 10.4324/9781003223313-50

In most cases we do not uncover near perfect images. It does not matter. If an image expresses the right concept to target consumers, e.g., high self-regard, accomplishment, consumers will select it. If you then ask them if they want to make any improvements to the image, the answer is invariably yes. Consumers will want the image to be brighter, the eyes to connect with someone, the setting in a different locale.

Our memory and imagination know what we want the image to convey to go from a good concept (why they picked it in the first place) to the ideal image in their mind. So, even without perfect images, we can learn, with the consumer's help, how to make it reflect their aspirations. Once they have their "improved" image, they can tell you how it makes them feel. And that feeling is the Desired Experience of our Brand Platform.

Chapter 44

Gathering Images for Research

We suggest you gather images for each element of the Brand Platform.

Fundamental Human Beliefs. Search for images that communicate the four questions that comprise the Beliefs:

■ Belonging. The winning image with Pampers was a mom and baby bonding, with the mom's eyes and the baby's eyes locked on each other. We had shown the new moms several mom and baby images, the winner expressed the concept of "skinship"…the physical and emotional bond between a mother and child that lasts a lifetime.

Belonging to beer drinkers might be the moment of connection when all the beer drinkers say cheers. Belonging might be a sports team celebrating a victory. The image also says accomplishment. Or what really matters is the connection between friends on the team.

There are a million bits of information in an image and the storytelling helps focus on the truth that really matters.

■ Mission. It could be a team working to solve a tough problem. They take pride in doing great work in and of itself. They take even greater pride in taking care of their families. Again, the storytelling gets at the essence. The image is the vehicle that opens the door into the consumer's mind…uncovering the Fundamental Beliefs that drove image selection.

DOI: 10.4324/9781003223313-51

- ■ Capability. The image selected by young boys about 11 or 12 was a boy pumping iron. The boys told us they loved their close buddies and wanted to experience things with them. Even more important was discovering who they are and who they want to be. Pumping iron was a symbol of working hard to accomplish something.
- ■ Identity. Identity is the most amorphous of the four questions and the most individual, i.e. less prone to stereotyping which we humans are programmed to do by evolution. Long before we had language, we needed to decide which group we belonged to, and the decision might have life and death consequences.

Identity answers Who Are You? We often ask consumers to search for 4–5 images that teach us Who You Are. The images they share with us help them to teach us their personal story. The story may be about their journey of self-discovery...a woman brought an image of an ad showing 32 flavors of ice cream. She said she was perceived as "mother wife" equivalent to "vanilla and chocolate" in the ad. She wanted to be seen for all the flavors... her many me's...not seen as only "mother wife."

Suggested exercise: The reader should gather 4–5 images to explain "Who Are You."

Once you have done so, select the image that is most important to you and tell yourself why. Then place the other images around the first image and explain their meaning and how they relate to the first image. The exercise will give you a hands-on feel for the way the image process yields important insight about your Fundamental Beliefs.

- ■ Desired Target Experience. You need to gather images that will tap into the targets' aspirations. As examples, first-time moms picked an image of a mom and her baby playing on the mom's bed. The image said the mom and baby were both loving and comfortable...the feeling that could lead to Skinship.

Potato chip lovers picked the four boys in the treehouse which was all about the kid in all of us.

Teenage girls looking at that picture said that their life was stressful as they had to push hard academically to create a path for success. How nice to be the age of the boys in the treehouse when your only job in life was to have fun.

Ore Ida moms picked the image of a family of four happily eating dinner together. When the moms got married, they dreamed of happy evening meals when everyone gathered to share their stories of the day. In real life, that happy dinner rarely happened. Interruptions, arguments, and absences were the reality. But their wish was to have that happy dinner.

That image became the Desired Experience for the Ore Ida Brand Platform.

Kroger shoppers selected an image of a family jogging on the beach. The image said the family was happy and healthy. That image became the Desired Experience of the Brand Platform.

■ Unique Advantage and Unique Advantage Support. The images that taught us about the targets' Fundamental Beliefs and Desired Experiences focus the development of Unique Advantage and Support.

We know that a new mom seeks Skinship and believes a loving and comfortable feeling creates the environment in which Skinship can happen (a stressed-out mom and/or a stressed out baby is not conducive to Skinship). With that insight in hand, we can hypothesize benefits...visual and verbal... that will link to those feelings.

Pampers wanted to support the baby's healthy growth and development so mom would have that comfortable and loving feeling that leads to Skinship. Babies develop rapidly over the first 18 months of life. The moms wanted newborns to sleep soundly and feed happily. Mom wanted to name a newborn diaper the "shh" diaper...a highly comforting feeling. The newborn diaper design is oversized for more comfort and named the Swaddler to communicate the benefit. The Cruiser diaper was designed with stretch materials to move with the toddler as she moved.

The Brand Platform is developed by "laddering down" from the target's Fundamental Belief and Desired Experience, both of which are about the target's life. We next need to develop a benefit that offers a unique advantage over existing alternatives. Part of the uniqueness will be functional and part emotional, i.e., delivering the feeling of the Desired Experience.

Chapter 45

Developing Verbal Benefits

Verbal Benefit Statements: How to Develop Benefits with the Potential to Deliver Unique Advantage

The goal: to develop benefit hypotheses with the potential to establish Unique Advantage.

In the previous chapter, we shared ideas about how to gather visuals for target audience research. Consumers' favorite images, i.e. images that tap into their beliefs and desired experiences, give us rich insight into tacit knowledge. And tacit knowledge helps populate key elements of the Brand Platform, importantly, Fundamental Human Beliefs and Desired Target Experience.

Written statements tend to be more functional or explicit and communicate a Brand's Unique Advantage and Unique Advantage Support. Statements can be a combination of rational and emotional elements.

To create these statements, I suggest the reader employ a few approaches described below:

- Category Benefit Structure. Established categories such as Carbonated Soft Drinks, Heavy Duty Detergents, and Cars and Trucks deliver an array of benefits that range from high, medium, to low importance in the consumer's mind.

You should tap into your own experience to begin gathering category benefits, e.g., Heavy Duty Detergent benefits…cleans every item in my laundry basket, removes stains, freshens, convenient to use, good value, not allergic,

DOI: 10.4324/9781003223313-52

works well in cold water etc. etc. Other sources of category benefits are competitive messaging, consumer reviews, primary research into category benefit structure.

A watch out. Categories are defined by companies and reflect their internal view of what constitutes a category. As such, these definitions can limit your thinking. To expand your thinking, check out the following two approaches.

■ Desired Target Experience. The favorite images selected by target consumers are a rich source of inspiration for benefit statement development. Pampers is a good example. New moms loved an image of a mom playing with her baby on her bed. The baby and mom are smiling. Both look very comfortable. The moms were asked to explain why the image was a favorite. Their answer: moms want to build bonds with their babies that will last a lifetime. The mom and baby image feels like a loving moment when the mom and baby are relaxed and unstressed...a perfect setting for physical and emotional bonding.

Moms went on to tell us they are always looking for ways to support their baby's development including evaluating whether products and services are helping them. Disposable diapers benefit – keeping babies drier than cloth diapers – was of little value to baby development.

The stories the moms told us – prompted by their favorite images – helped us expand our thinking about category benefits. In the case of Pampers, could a disposable diaper have a role in a baby's healthy growth and development. If so, that would be a new benefit for the category.

A diaper benefit was created to support a baby's healthy growth and development. The benefit was an ideal or desired experience for a diaper. Moms told us that no diaper at the time could deliver that benefit but, if it could, that would be a game changer. The lesson here is to listen to the target's wishes – it's the best clue about the future they desire. Benefits should explore how to deliver today's category benefits better..."what is"...and benefits new to the category..."what might be."

Analogies, Metaphors, Archetypes

Analogies. It's valuable to check out brands in other categories that have changed the rules of the game. The cola market offered a relevant analogy for potato chips.

Cola is a mainstream market. The leaders – Coke and Pepsi – have loyal customers and charge premium prices. The leaders delivered a highly desirable taste experience and aspirational emotional benefits about happiness, success, and connection. Could potato chips deliver branded benefits that move the leaders – in our case, Lays – from a commodity to a value added, premium brand? With colas and beverages in general, there was a belief in "image taste transfer" – a beverage could create an aspirational image in its messaging – and consumers' would "drink" the image. Could the same be true for a product we eat? The Lay's Brand Hypothesis was a test of whether the analogy with cola was feasible.

Metaphors. Target consumers told us potato chips are harmony when they selected an image of a family get together where all ages were happy together. Potato chips are a key ingredient creating a happy family get together because potato chips are a simple pleasure. And simple pleasures connect us all. The metaphor opened the door to the emotional benefits of potato chips.

Archetypes. Over several years, Godiva had lost its magic. The brand was seen as a safe corporate gift...something a boss gives to her assistant at Christmas. Godiva had a perceived value and, as such, was a nice way to say thank you for a job well done. The Godiva buyers had aged, and sales were declining. Godiva was not winning younger consumers entering the market.

To young, chocolate loving prospects, chocolate is passion, and the chocolate experience should reflect that passion.

Two archetypes inspired brand building hypotheses...the Lover and the Creator. The Lover guides messaging, and the Creator guided product innovation.

Benefit statements give us a way to explore all the ways a brand can change a consumer's life for the better. We need to generate the widest and deepest benefits to crack the code to crack the Brand Platform code.

Chapter 46

Three Money Making Strategies

What Are the Three Money Making Strategies?

It's helpful to consider which of three types of money making strategies best suits the new brand we are creating.

- Brands such as Tide, Toyota, Google, Visa are Mainstream Brand leaders. These brands usually "own" the main benefit(s) that drive a category, e.g. Tide owns clean, Toyota owns reliability, Google owns breadth and speed of search, Visa owns utility (accepted everywhere).
- Segmented Brands such as American Express. Mercedes, Rolex have selected a specific target consumer, in this case, upscale consumers who are willing and able to pay a premium for a premium experience. Markets can, of course, be segmented many ways, e.g. by lifestyle, cohort, age, passion. The point is that segmented brands choose not to compete in the broad, mainstream market.
- Price Brands such as Walmart, Costco, Amazon who seek to deliver the benefits consumers seek at a lower price. Their low cost operator position gives them the ability to deliver low cost benefits and make money in the process.

The PIMS database places perspective on the three money making strategies. PIMS (Profit Impact of Market Strategies) is a comprehensive, long-term study of the performance of strategic business units in 3000 companies. The

DOI: 10.4324/9781003223313-53

goal is to determine which business strategies make the difference between success and failure.

A key conclusion from the study: two factors...share and quality...drive ROI.

Mainstream leaders deliver superior quality to a broad base of category users. Price brands deliver lower prices to a broad base of users. Segmented leaders deliver superior quality to a specific group of category customers. Segmented leaders can increase ROI if they can win a larger share of the segment they serve.

The book will contain a Brand Book available in electronic and hard copy formats that enables the reader to input his/her ideas/content for each step of the process.

- ■ I will be available via my website to answer questions and evaluate brand solutions.

Chapter 47

Personal Brands

I've suggested the reader bring the process alive by applying to a brand of interest. Creating the reader's personal brand is another way to experience the approach.

You would start by setting goals for your personal brand. Your goals may be to entertain...to make people happy...to achieve personal or professional growth...to inspire societal change.

Once your goals are set, you would apply the Foundation Stage steps:

- build your Business Framework with insights about your target audience, your capabilities, competitive landscape...all the elements that capture the big picture world in which your personal brand will operate.
- you will seek metaphors, analogies, and archetypes to inspire brand hypotheses development.

For example, what can you learn about Tony Robbins, Oprah, Elon Musk, or other successful personal brand builders that might be instructive? What do they stand for? How and where do they tell their brand story?

- you will conduct research with the target audience to learn about their beliefs and aspirations.

Whom do they admire and why? You will explore a range of benefits of your personal brand, i.e., how your brand will change their life for the better.

- you will develop the Brand Platform that links the most motivating benefits of your personal brand with the Beliefs and Desired Experience of your target audience.
- you will move on to the Conceptualization Stage creating a Brand Concept that brings your Brand Platform to life. You will ask for feedback on your concept from your target audience.
- you will develop the elements to implement your personal brand platform in messaging, design, digital media. You will codify your platform in your Brand Purpose and Brand Vision templates.

The personal brand platform may be an efficient way to learn the process. Most of the information needed to apply the process is readily available and, given the brand is you, the emotional truths are in your memory and imagination.

Chapter 48

Helping the Reader Own the Process

My wish is to make the book a laboratory for readers...a place to experience the process, not just read about it...adults learn by doing. To that end, I'm suggesting the readers interact with the content from the get-go by:

- capturing their perceptions about branding and desired outcomes from the book at the outset...a benchmark to evaluate progress in learning the process and fulfilling expectations
- applying the process with a brand of their choice...a corporate brand, their personal brand...to bring the learning experience to life
- interacting with me via email to answer any questions along the way
- reading the book together with other readers...a brand building book club of sorts...to create a collaborative experience. Engaging senior management to gain feedback and demonstrate value.

Further, to make the experience as real as possible, the book is organized into sections to bring the process to life from several vantage points:

- where did the process come from...the early history that led to the Success Model and Method
- what are the elements of the process...what is the role of each stage and each step with the stage
- why does the process work...why is it proven and why is it effective

DOI: 10.4324/9781003223313-55

- what case histories demonstrate the overall success of the process and the stages and steps that helped shape that success
- what consultants who worked for me learned from the process...I view the consultants as reader surrogates. They had to learn the process, apply it and decide whether to become believers
- what my clients believe about branding initiatives in general and managing my process with their internal teams and stakeholders. My branding experience is all from the consulting side of the equation. Senior client management is focused on gaining alignment and commitment from their internal audience required to implement the process with success. As such, they need to deal with the systems and culture of organizations which can often raise substantial executional barriers. Their insights about the process, i.e., the politics and bureaucratic beliefs that are often not in sync with risks of implementing a creative concept
- what can be learned from other fields such as AI and gaming that validate my brand building process and the creative process broadly considered.

Chapter 49

Pitfalls and Watchouts

When does the process not work?

What are the barriers to success?

1) Brand Platform Execution. Failure to translate the Platform into motivating messaging and design. This may happen if we did not engage all stakeholders...internally and externally...into the process.

   Some stakeholders do not feel they have a stake in the outcome or feel committed to another, perhaps legacy, brand story.

   The team feels the need to act against a particular timeline the project could not accommodate...the infamous timeline driver.

   The company's KPIs do not measure emotional benefits. "You get what you measure" and if you only measure functional benefits, you can't prove the power of the Platform to drive performance.

2) Senior Management Involvement. Management may not stop the process from going forward but they may not believe in branding or believe it can make a big difference.

   "Branding is naming." Branding is design vs Branding can establish long-term competitive advantage...give the organization a sense of purpose...change people's lives for the better.

   Most senior managers I've worked with believe in the power of branding before we embark on a project. The risk they are taking is whether this process will succeed.

DOI: 10.4324/9781003223313-56

When executives do not have shared beliefs about branding, the odds of success go down. These managers need to be educated by the project team to improve the chances of winning. Sometimes an uphill battle because they have not had success with brand building initiatives.

Susan Sanderson Briggs found a way to minimize the lack of brand understanding among the senior management in the retail sector in which she operates. She never described the process as branding. Her management believed in the power of operations to drive success. Susan described the project to make operational improvements which fit management's world view. "Would a rose by any other name smell as sweet?"

3) Corporate Culture and Systems. Managers meet performance objectives by applying the principles and procedures prescribed by their company. They are rewarded for making the systems operate smoothly and effectively. Brand building projects are complex creative projects which require the discovery and application of new knowledge. They often require taking big risks. The manager mentality is not comfortable with projects of this nature and should not be asked to manage them. When they do, the results can be sub-optimal.

A few managers see themselves as leaders. And those of us who work with them feel the difference leaders can make on creative projects. They do not delegate. They know the importance of their involvement. They know the project must uncover an insight which will underpin a Platform. The insight must be translated into forms the organization can understand. The measurement systems must be capable of evaluating emotional content.

Time needs to be given to ensure the Platform is translated into messaging that motivates all stakeholders.

Chapter 50

Treat Others with Respect

The most important guiding principle of my Success Model is to treat people with respect...your core target audience, your co-workers, your stakeholders. When we respect others, we open the door to an enduring relationship.

I've seen this principle brought home in many ways. Peter Drucker, the management guru, who inspired several generations of leaders, stated that the most important quality management should display is "tolerance and goodwill." Bob Iger's book, *The Ride of a Lifetime*, offers example after example of the power of respect. Bob's respect for Steve Jobs led to the Pixar acquisition. Respect for Roy Disney helped Bob's transition to Disney CEO and avoided a lawsuit. Respect for George Lucas led to the acquisition of Lucas films. An ego trip would have undermined all the above. Bob's direct reports were always treated with dignity which in turn encouraged them to treat their people with dignity.

I suspect we may have a self-respect gene gratis of evolution. We sense how others feel about us regardless of their words. At one point in our ancient history, survival may have depended on whom we choose to trust.

Donna Hicks wrote a book, *Dignity: The Essential Role It Plays in Resolving Conflict*. Donna works with a group at Harvard that helps opposing parties resolve conflict, e.g. Israel vs Palestine. The bottom line...the successful resolution of seemingly intractable conflict results when both parties feel the other side respects them.

FDR's brain trust had one goal with their New Deal initiatives. Help Americans regain their dignity.

The Brand Platform must answer the question: what does this brand say about me? If the answer is that the brand values you and respects what you stand for, the opportunity for an enduring relationship is at hand.

DOI: 10.4324/9781003223313-57

Chapter 51

Learning Skills

Academic institutions want students to develop an array of skills that will be highly valued in the marketplace. A few of the skills are discussed below as they all relate to successful brand building.

Active Listening is defined as attentive listening, including "listening" to non-verbal clues, paraphrasing, and making no judgments. Our company trained our moderators to never introduce their views into the conversations to avoid leader bias. They were also instructed to paraphrase respondent comments as a way of determining if the moderator understood what respondents were teaching us. Nonverbal communication is the most important way we interpret what people feel about something. Body language doesn't lie.

We suggest people attending a focus group write down what respondents are saying...take lots of notes...not just summarize a key insight. The reason: the insights from respondents are usually coming in at a rapid pace...at a faster pace than can be absorbed and analyzed on the spot. Reviewing lots of notes after a session helps with the analysis...time to think through what the session taught us about our target and our brand hypotheses. Taking notes is most applicable to understanding the meaning of an image respondents selected. A sentence may contain 10–20 bits of information. An image has a million bits of information.

A client once told me the basis for our success...we listened so intently. Active Listening is a highly valuable skill.

DOI: 10.4324/9781003223313-58

- ■ Fluency of Ideas. The ability to generate lots of ideas. I'm not sure it's a teachable skill but it is certainly a highly valued skill. When we are in the divergent mode, i.e., when we are generating ideas, we should keep generating them even when we have been doing so for a while (and are a bit sick of it). After that we should go on to generate some more ideas. People who are highly creative will contribute the most to this generative exercise. The size or scope of a given idea is not important in the divergent phase...quantity of ideas is most important. Quantity helps in a few ways. The most important for me is that a given idea may spark another idea from another participant in the process. "Can I build on your idea" is usually a great way to expand creative thinking... on an individual or team level.
- ■ Inductive Reasoning and Deductive Reasoning. Inductive reasoning develops a theory. Deductive reasoning tests a theory. Our brand building process was developed by inductive reasoning. We developed the theory of the Success Model from the specific truths of the Jif and Downy cases. Deductive reasoning was applied to test the theory via evidence from the brand building with our clients.
- ■ Complex Problem Solving. When goals are vague or hard to reach via routine actions, complex problem solving comes into play. From my experience, the creative process is a synonym for complex problem solving.

A rich deep knowledge base is required as is a collaborative (cross-functional) team. Our brand building process goes through stages and steps which, taken in concert, solve the problem of creating a brand proposition that will: create Unique Advantage, be competitively insulated, and drive growth over long periods of time.

The process is designed to avoid the "poke and hope" approach to brand building. Particularly when creating a new brand effectively puts us in the "hit" business...and most new initiatives fail.

EXPANDING THE LENS

Chapter 52

David Brooks. *NYTimes* Columnist

David recently wrote a column, "This Is How the Truth Dies," that addresses the sources of knowledge that underpin the brand building process.

David's subject is the two kinds of knowledge that enable great nations to thrive. One source is about a nation's identity…who we are, how we got here, what binds us together, what kind of world we want to build together. David characterizes this truth as emotional and moral.

The second kind of knowledge David describes as propositional knowledge. We acquire this knowledge "through reason, logical proof and tight analysis. Evidence-based knowledge…how the scientific revolution expanded what we believe to be true and can prove to be true.

We humans are emotional creatures…we desire…we feel…and our feelings lead to actions. The knowledge that guides nations is gained through "emotional experiences–stories."

The Brand Platform combines the two kinds of knowledge into one holistic story. Fundamental Human Beliefs and Desired Experiences are about the emotional truths of an individual or group of individuals (target audience). The Unique Advantage and Unique Advantage Support must link to Beliefs and Desired Experiences to be meaningful and motivating.

David wants to heal a nation and believes we will only come together when we can find one emotional story about our identity that is inclusive and inspiring. It would be a great application of the brand building process if it could be used to bind a nation together. The process was designed for brands…but why not nations.

DOI: 10.4324/9781003223313-60

The French have a word for the process of bringing people with sharply different beliefs together…charrette, the process in which all stakeholders in a project attempt to resolve conflicts and map solutions. The underlying assumption is that the human quality of empathy kicks in when we hear the views of others…even diametrically opposing views or emotionally based fears.

Chapter 53

A Peek into the Future

Neuroscience is beginning to understand why and how we humans create meaning. The learning helps provide deeper insight into why the brand building process is valid. And, on a much more significant level, open pathways for humans to create a more just, tolerant, and empathetic society.

The human brain is considered the most complex organ ever created and is the least understood by science. Harvard University has created the Brain Science Institute to unite all brain science research under one umbrella, believing that brain research will yield more fruitful new knowledge than any other field of study.

I noted earlier that positive psychology insights have impacted our understanding of the way humans operate...we should be called Homo Prospectus given how we use memory and imagination to navigate the world. We are always exploring possible new paths or ideas ultimately selecting the path we should take to meet our objectives...objectives ranging from what to eat for lunch to where to live, take a job, or retire.

The branding process incorporates positive psychology to gain insight into our desired experiences, i.e., what we wish to happen in the future to realize our hopes and dreams.

Neuroscience hypothesizes that the brain is a hierarchical system and the highest parts of our brain, developed late in evolution, seek to manage the lower parts of our brain that house emotion and memory. The higher parts of the brain are where our sense of self is created as we move into adulthood. Our sense of self or ego or self-interest is a code for making decisions in our best interests. When emotions might take us off track, our ego inhibits our emotions.

DOI: 10.4324/9781003223313-61

The good news is that the code helps us manage the massive array of stimuli that comes at us every minute. The bad news is that we are not open to explore and discover new ideas.

Children whose brains are not yet coded are much more open to discover. I wrote earlier about the power of the right brain over the left brain... for the logic and analysis of the right to shut down the emotional left brain.

Betty Edwards' book, *Drawing on the Right Side of the Brain*, gives us a real world way to experience left brain dominance. When she is teaching students to learn how to draw, she finds they are inhibited by the left brain dominance. The left brain discourages our drawing efforts, criticizing our efforts as juvenile ("you can't draw"). Of greater consequence, the left brain does not let us perceive the subject of our drawing. One trick she offers is to turn the picture we want to draw upside down. When we do this, the left brain shuts down and seems to say "I have no way to make sense of that upside down picture so I'll just ignore it." The trick works...I tried it...it allowed me to perceive the lines and spaces of the picture purely without interruption from the left brain boss.

Neuroscience studies have experimented with mushrooms that seem to have the power to reduce or eliminate ego from consciousness. The default mode network that houses our ego is quieted. Duality...our ego and the outside world...stops operating. People who participate in these studies feel another sense of consciousness...sometimes spiritual, sometimes love, sometimes less fear or anxiety.

If we humans are meaning making creatures, the early implications of neuroscience are potential ways to expand our consciousness that will enable us to create new stories. And if you are an optimist like me, maybe these new stories will move us to better ways to manage our lives and the world we live in. And maybe the unscientific teachings of Buddhism, Freud, Jung, the Aztecs et al. may ultimately have some scientific validation.

There is already promise that addiction, mental illness, and anxiety (at its most extreme, fear of death) can be assuaged. Addiction, mental illness, and anxiety have a common mental trait...the inability to get beyond the ego-driven, self-destructive story of their lives. Mushrooms and other techniques (breathing therapies) lessen ego dominance which, in turn, expands the mind's ability to discover and explore new stories and not be trapped in the ego-driven story rut.

Chapter 54

Artificial Intelligence

Rene Bunnel worked in Silicon Valley as a technologist. She later studied for her PhD in psychology. By the time we met a few years ago, she had created Emoto-AI, an artificial intelligence service that helps brands build deeper relationships with their target audience.

Her psychological training included the study of positive psychology. A brief detour into the mission of positive psychology. Positive psychology is a reaction to the psychology practiced in the 1960s and 1970s which was focused on pathologies, i.e. what is wrong with people, why are they mentally disturbed or deficient.

Positive psychology comes from the opposite premise. What's right about people? What are their character strengths and virtues? And how their character strength helps them live happier, more fulfilling lives. One other distinction between positive and (pardon the expression) negative psychology – the psychologists in the 1960s and 1970s viewed themselves as humanists who did not trust science as the appropriate discipline for psychological research. In many ways, they illustrate C. P. Snow's Two Cultures ... humanities and science that fail to talk with each other or trust each other.

Positive psychology seeks to develop the science of human strengths. To that end, they developed 24-character traits that have been validated in research conducted over decades.

Examples of character traits include prudence, spirituality, open-mindedness, love of learning, love, creativity, hope, humility, leadership, humor.

Most of us have about three character traits that are disproportionately important to defining who we are. Once we can identify these strengths, they can help guide us as we navigate our lives.

DOI: 10.4324/9781003223313-62

The premise, to use a marketing term, is market to strength. Apply your character strengths to make your world and the world a better place.

So what's all this got to do with branding? Rene Bunnel created Emoto AI, a human centered algorithm that analyzed character traits of consumer segments and brands that wanted to build or deepen a connection with them. Brands have character traits which once identified can be matched with consumer segments. The results of the AI analysis are a way for brands to tell stories that reflect character traits held in common.

Like Fundamental Human Beliefs, character traits are universal, create meaning and motivate our behavior.

On one level, character traits research is another way to validate my brand building process.

Each process seeks universal truths to build connections. On another level, positive psychology broadly and character strengths specifically show promise about ways science can expand the brand building tool box and its moral compass.

Does the process need to be so time consuming? To date, yes. It's often years to identify, develop, test, and execute a new Brand Platform. Are there any signs the process can be streamlined without losing effectiveness? I think so. A book by Marco Iansiti and Karim Lakhani, *Competing in the Age of AI*, gives us a few clues.

The book describes how companies like Apple, Google, and Moderna have built organizations based on an integrated, exponential system guided by data centric scientific reasoning. This model is in sharp contrast to the traditional model which is a siloed system that does not communicate across the enterprise. These companies use the predictive power of AI.

The issue at hand is whether AI can be applied to accelerate the brand building process.

The Covid pandemic is instructive. The crisis gave companies like Moderna the opportunity to create a vaccine in record time. Their operating platform engaged all people involved in the solution with accurate, timely data to inform their decisions.

Even traditional companies like IKEA, Novartis, and Mass General employed AI systems to accelerate patient care in the face of the pandemic.

I've mentioned the work Emoto AI has done to apply psychology (the human side of enterprise) to AI algorithms (character traits) for brand building purposes.

Applying AI with the brand building process seems to offer a few advantages that include:

- target definition, competitive landscape, product development/ prototyping, measurement.
- shared knowledge across the enterprise. A branding project would be less a silo undertaking but understood and supported by the organization broadly.
- interacting with me at my book's website: howtobuildyourbrand.net

Competing in the Age of AI is a recent book by two Harvard Business School professors. It's about the success of Apple, Netflix, Google, and Moderna who have created an integrated operating system based on data centric scientific reasoning.

The advantage over traditional silo-based companies is substantial.

There are many implications for branding opportunities. For example, Netflix can easily expand its entertainment brand to compete against games and social media brands like YouTube and Tik Tok. Netflix wants a greater share of the time we spend entertaining ourselves. YouTube and Fortnite et al. control many hours of our time. Netflix AI-based operating system gives them easy access to those categories. A fact our Capabilities factor in our Business Framework must consider.

In the entertainment industry the rallying cry was always "content is king." Netflix might counter with "distribution is king kong."

Chapter 55

Why Startups Fail: Lessons from Startups

Tom Eisenmannn's book, *Why Startups Fail,* has relevant insight for branding failures. Harvard Business School where Tom teaches defines entrepreneurship as "pursuing novel opportunities while lacking resources. Entrepreneurs must create and deliver something new – a solution to a customer's problem that's better than or costs less than, current options."

That definition applies to a brand building initiative. Brand initiatives, like startups, must manage four risks:

Demand Risk: do prospects see the benefits of the new opportunity? Are they motivated to buy? Is there a large enough prospect pool to meet the financial goals of the branding venture? These questions require a thoughtful process to identify the core target. And there are false fronts to watch out for...sometimes a small group of early adopters may make a purchase. Early adopters often have a set of motivations including to be the first on their block to buy in that is not representative of the prospect pool broadly defined. The onus is on the brand team to identify and confirm the size and mindset of target prospects to avoid the Demand Risk mistake.

R&D Risk: can we crack the code on the product solution? Do we know technological or engineering barriers that need to be overcome to have a viable solution. Our product must exceed target prospects' expectations. We should not green light a project until we have evidence that we have done so.

DOI: 10.4324/9781003223313-63

Implementation Risk: do we have the right team to increase the odds of success in the marketplace? Is the team committed to the Brand Platform and able to develop and deploy the executional elements to ensure the opportunity is realized in the marketplace?

Financial Risk: is the branding project properly funded? I was part of a team who launched Gain, a heavy-duty detergent developed by Procter & Gamble. We had studied the laundry detergent buyers to determine if we had a sufficiently large prospect pool. We assumed no business would come from consumers who wanted to buy a low-priced detergent; they did not believe there was any difference between lower and higher priced brands. We assumed little or no volume from Tide users who were extremely loyal to that brand. We did assume some volume from consumers who were buying specialty detergents designed for cold water washing.

However, our expectations were modest because "cold water" washing had not yet achieved a meaningful volume.

We did assume we could attract laundry consumers who evaluated clean laundry by its scent.

We had data on the number of consumers who love the smell of clean laundry. We also had data on the strong preference for our scent in blind test studies.

Gain was one of the first detergents that could remove stains like grass and blood. We knew this was an important new benefit that gave us superiority over conventional detergents that could only remove dirt. P&G had initially wanted to launch Gain without the costly stain removal ingredient. We recommended testing the two formulations to determine consumer preference. The stain removal formula was a blind test winner and justified premium pricing.

Our positioning proclaimed that Gain Treats Stains Like Dirt. We didn't want to communicate that Gain was a specialty product for stains. We wanted Gain to be perceived as appropriate and superior for all wash loads.

We invested heavily in a door-to-door sampling program giving prospects the opportunity to sample Gain for several wash loads. There were a number of other, less costly sampling programs, e.g., a coupon for a free box of Gain. Experience with other brand introductions taught us that the trial and conversion of prospects to users was much stronger via door-to-door sampling vs all other sampling programs. The lesson here was that the most expensive sampling program was the cheapest way to build a brand. Door to door sampling built a large sustainable franchise. A cheaper sampling program would have built a smaller business. And you don't get a second chance to make a good first impression.

Gain faced Demand, R&D, Implementation and Financial risks. Had we made the wrong decisions in any of these areas, we could have had a failure on our hands. It's true that P&G had a vast reservoir of detergent market data and experience. They also had a low risk tolerance; their motto: we'd rather be second and right. Nonetheless, the risks of failure need to be addressed.

Chapter 56

Where the Process Fits in the Corporate Landscape: Positioning the Process

How do brand driven companies position Lubin Lawrence in the consulting landscape?

Management consulting firms analyze the past. Their source of knowledge is historical data. If, for example, a company wants to analyze global promotion practices of a given industry, management consultants are engaged. The output of their analysis is a strategy supported by data analysis.

Exceptionally focused firms such as ad agencies, digital marketing, and designers approach their projects conceptually. Their output is execution that brings a company's strategy to life.

The Lubin Lawrence process is strategic and conceptual. Our task is to create the future.

When our work is completed, executional firms are engaged to implement the solution.

In many ways, the book is to teach companies a process that will help them manage the organization as it seeks to move from today to tomorrow.

DOI: 10.4324/9781003223313-64

Chapter 57

From Brand Purpose to Corporate Purpose

Brand Purpose expresses how a brand changes the life of a consumer for the better. Pampers' Brand Purpose was to support a baby's healthy growth and development. The statement helped Pampers move beyond a functional, undifferentiated "keeps baby drier" to an aspirational role in the mom's and baby's life. With Pampers' success, P&G encouraged all brand teams to develop their brand's purpose.

Today, a new generation of employees are encouraging their companies to state and realize the larger purpose for which the company is in business. In the past, company purpose or value statements were created inside the company. And the source of the statement was usually the C suite.

The impetus is now bottom up for employees who want to be proud to go to work for their company. For that to happen, the company must address societal issues like climate change and equity for all employees. Employees will choose companies with values they share.

Consumers increasingly expect companies to deliver societal value beyond shareholder value.

The pandemic has only amplified this aspiration. It's also becoming increasingly clear that the government alone cannot address the broad array of complex problems that countries around the world now face.

All the above expands and deepens the role of brand building. A brand's competitive landscape was usually focused on direct and indirect competitors. The landscape must now embrace global citizenship.

DOI: 10.4324/9781003223313-65

Chapter 58

Keep Your Competition Close and Your Consumer Closer

Disney chose to distribute *Black Widow* simultaneously in theatres and streaming on Disney+.

Scarlett Johansson was not very happy with that distribution plan as it may have deprived her of a substantial share of theatrical revenues. Disney would also lose money by not focusing 100% on theatrical release.

Why would Disney behave the way it did? The easy answer is the opportunity for Disney to expand its consumer base for Disney+.

The other reason was speculated upon by *Marketing Week*, a UK marketing journal. They contend that theatre distributors have direct access to Disney movie customers. Streaming gives Disney direct access to its customers. Disney can learn who bought Black Widow, why, and what else they bought. More to the point, Disney can now have an ongoing relationship with its consumers to direct all future initiatives.

Distributors like Tesco, Amazon, Target, and Walmart have direct consumer contact. That helps them gain an advantage vs their branded suppliers where the relationship is indirect. Disney is seeking to change the equation.

At the heart of the brand building process is rich consumer insight. We need to author a strong brand story. That story can only pay off if we keep our consumer close.

DOI: 10.4324/9781003223313-66   **171**

Keep Your Competition Close and Your Career Closer

Appendix: Tools of the Research Process

Research Design and Screener

Following is a list of the data we will need to develop the Research Design and Screener:

1. Based on segments we choose, e.g., fans, high potentials, mid potentials): How are these segments defined? What are the essentials for an individual to be considered part of this segment? What would exclude an individual from being considered part of this segment? What differentiates the segments?
2. What are the key questions? For example, they must use the internet at least once a day (terminate if once a week).
3. What are the demographics of the users? For example, race/ethnicity, HHI, education level, household composition, etc.

Respondent Specs & Research Design
Group Mix:
Race & Ethnicity: Mix, skew Caucasian (50% Caucasian, 50% Hispanic/Latino, and/or African American)
Gender & Sex: Mixed
Education: Partial college or higher
Completely fluent in English
HHI: high low income to middle income (based on market)
Mid-to-high household use of internet

DOI: 10.4324/9781003223313-67

At least slight awareness of cord-cutting/OTT

Open to new services

"Decision Makers": pay the bills, choose utility services, awareness of different utility makers, concern about price & quality of service, provider position for self and others in household

	HH Decision Makers 25–35	HH Decision Makers 36–50
Fans	X	X
High Potentials	X	X
Mid Potentials	X	X

Screeners

Recruiter: Ask to speak to member of household in charge of utilities and bills.

Hello, my name is_____from [   ], a local market research company. Today we are conducting a short survey and we would like to include your opinions.

Please be assured that we are not selling anything now or in the future as a result of this study. If you fit the profile of one of our research segments and are interested in participating, you will be invited to take part in one of the market research group discussions we are conducting in your area [relevant dates].

Refreshments will be served and you will be paid for sharing your time and views with us.

Is this a convenient time to ask you a few questions?

Yes 1   **CONTINUE**

No 2   **ESTABLISH MUTUALLY CONVENIENT TIME TO CALL BACK**

1. What is your age?_____

RECRUITER: Recruit respondents with the following ages:

2a. Which of the following best describes you? **(READ)**

White/Caucasian
Black/African American
Native American
Asian American
Hispanic or Latino
Other_____

RECRUITER: Recruit respondents to have a mix of Caucasian/White, African American, and Hispanic/Latino.

2b. Are you of Hispanic or Latino descent?

Yes
No

3a. Are you or any member of your family currently employed, or have you or any member of your family been employed in the past, in any of the following types of businesses or occupations? **(READ)**

1. Advertising or Marketing (Including Internet companies)
2. The Advertising or Marketing department of a company
3. Market Research or Sales Promotion
4. Public relations/Graphic Design
5. Any type of media: radio/television/newspaper/magazine or media website
6. Internet Services
7. Television or Entertainment

RECRUITER: Terminate if respondent answers "yes" to any of the above.

3b. Are you or any member of your family currently employed or have been employed in the past by any of the following companies? **(READ)**

RECRUITER: Terminate if any employment (currently or in the past) (self or member of family) by any company listed above.

4a. When was the last time, if ever, you participated in a market research group discussion or one-on-one in-depth interview or with a market research company?

RECRUITER: DO NOT READ.

Within the past 6 months	1	**TERMINATE**
Longer than 6 months ago	2	**ASK Q4b/4c/4d**
Never	3	**SKIP TO Q5a**

RECRUITER: Terminate any market research in the past 6 months.

4b. How many market research group discussions or one-on-one in-depth interviews have you ever participated in?

_____

RECRUITER: No more than 3 groups/one-on-ones ever.

4c. What was/were the subject(s) of the market research group discussion(s) or one-on-one in-depth interviews in which you have participated? What others? **(ASK FOR ALL)**

_____

_____

4d. Have you ever participated in a market research group discussion or one-on-one in-depth interview about ... **(READ)**

Internet Services	Yes	No	**If yes, TERM**
Television Services	Yes	No	**If yes, TERM**
Electric Services	Yes	No	
Heat and Gas Services	Yes	No	

5a. What utilities does your current household use?

Internet Services	Yes	No	**If no, TERM**
Television Services	Yes	No	**If no, TERM**
Electric Services	Yes	No	
Heat and Gas Services	Yes	No	

5b. Who choses your utility providers for your current household?
_____ Pre-chosen by building management*
_____ Chosen by other person in household*
_____ Chosen by a mix of people in the household*
_____ I chose the majority of the utility providers
_____ I chose all of the utility providers
RECRUITER: Terminate if respondent selects (*)

6b. How did you choose your utility providers?
_____ Based on price*
_____ Based on brand awareness
_____ Based on reviews
_____ Based on deals from utility providers
RECRUITER: Terminate if respondent selects (*)

6c. Which of the following best describes your responsibility for handling your household's utility bills?
_____ I am responsible for handling all or almost all of my household's utility bills
_____ I am responsible for handling at least half of my household's utility bills
_____ I am responsible for handling less than half of my household's utility bills*
_____ I am not responsible for handling my household's utility bills *
RECRUITER: Terminate if respondent selects (*)

7a. Which of the following best describes your responsibility for choosing new household products and services?
_____ Chosen by other person in household*
_____ Chosen by a mix of people in the household*
_____ I chose the majority of the household products and services
_____ I chose all of the household products and services

RECRUITER: Terminate if respondent selects (*)

7b. How do you chose your household products and services?

_____ Based on price*

_____ Based on brand awareness

_____ Based on reviews

_____ Based on deals

RECRUITER: Terminate if respondent selects (*)

8a. Which of the following statements best describes approximately how much time you use the internet each day (on computers, laptops, mobile phones, or other devices) **(READ)**

Constantly	**CONTINUE**
Every hour	**CONTINUE**
Every few hours	**CONTINUE**
When I need to	**TERMINATE**
Every few days	**TERMINATE**
At least once a week	**TERMINATE**
	TERMINATE

8b. What do you use the internet for? **(READ)**

To browse social media	**YES**	**NO**
To answer/send email	**YES**	**NO**
For personal research	**YES**	**NO**
For business/work	**YES**	**NO**
For school	**YES**	**NO**
To watch content on YouTube	**YES**	**NO (TERM)**
To watch streaming services like Netflix, Hulu, or Amazon Prime	**YES**	**NO**

RECRUITER: Respondents must use the internet for at least 3+ of the options **AND** must watch YouTube.

9. In a typical month, how many times do you, personally, socialize with friends, family? Would you say that you socialize with friends …?
(READ)

Once a month or less frequently	1	**TERMINATE**
Two to three times a month	2	
Or, four or more times a month	3	

RECRUITER: Recruit a mix.

10. What is your marital status? Are you ... **(READ)**
    Married
    Single, living with significant other
    Single, living alone
    Widowed
    Divorced/separated
RECRUITER: Recruit a mix.

11. Which of the following describes your employment status? Are you ...
    (READ)

Self-employed full-time	1	SKIP TO Q 15b
Self-employed part-time	2	**TERMINATE**
Employed full-time – 40 or more hours per week	3	ASK Q 15a&b
Employed part-time	4	**TERMINATE**
Unemployed	6	**TERMINATE**
Retired	7	**TERMINATE**

12a. By what company are you employed?_____

12b. What is your occupation?_____

RECRUITER: Aim for _____.

Q12A AND Q12B ARE DOUBLE CHECKS TO SECURITY FROM Q3A&B.

13. Into which of the following categories does your total household
    income fall? **(READ)**

Under $30,000	1	TERMINATE
$30,000 – $44,000	2	TERMINATE
$45,000 – $69,000	3	TERMINATE
$70,000 – $84,000	4	
$85,000 – $99,000	5	
$100,000+	6	
Refused	7	TERMINATE

RECRUITER: Household income must be $100,000+. Recruit a mix.

14. What was the last grade of school you had the opportunity to complete?
    Was it ... **(READ)**

Some high school	1	**TERMINATE**
Completed high school	2	**TERMINATE**
Trade school/other specialized training after high school	3	**TERMINATE**
Some college	4	**TERMINATE**
Completed college	5	
Some post graduate	6	
Masters degree	7	
Ph.D. degree	8	

RECRUITER: Respondents must have completed high school (at least). Recruit a mix.

15. Now a question just for fun. In 4 to 5 sentences, please describe what famous person, dead or alive, would you like to have dinner with?

RECRUITER: This is an open-ended articulation question. While screening these people, you are monitoring how quickly they respond to the statements, how verbal they are, and how intelligent their answers are. Please listen carefully to both the quality of the respondent's voice (if he/she mumbles, has a heavy accent, etc.) and the quality of the content (sounds intelligent, makes sense, not too repetitive). Respondent must speak clearly, provide an articulate response, and be enthusiastic to qualify.

I'd like to invite you to participate in a group discussion. The session will last approximately two and a half hours and you will be required to complete a homework assignment prior. You will be paid $_____ for your time. Would you like to attend it?

If you have any questions prior to the research, please do not hesitate to call _____ at _____. Someone from our offices will call you again prior to the day of the research to confirm your attendance.

Leader's Guide Outline

	KEY EXERCISES	*PURPOSE/OUTPUT*
PRE-WORK	Homework: Imagery Gathered at Home	– Identity: "Who are you?" – Imagery of how they see Google Fiber and/or key competitors today
	Benefits Selection	– Respondents privately select Fundamental Values and Google Fiber benefits prior to the session
	Warm Up/ Introduction	– Respondents' background
SESSION FORMAT	Discuss "Homework"	– What do the images teach us about … – Who they are? – The competitive landscape of Internet, TV, and/or phone service today, and what they wish could become in the better
	Mission	– Respondents create the most ideal Internet, TV, and phone service
	Value Benefit Evaluation	–Understand Fundamental Values that motivate consumers
	Visual Exploratory	– Understand consumers' desired experiences in life and with their Internet, TV, and/or phone service provider
	Unique Advantage Evaluation	– Identify unique and leverageable benefits for an Internet, TV, and phone service provider
	Clustering Exercise	– Develop the holistic vision that is emotionally compelling and "different in kind" for an ideal Internet, TV, and phone service provider
	Summation Exercise	– Why is this vision unique and ideal, and what does Google Fiber have to do to deliver this ideal?

Leader's Guide

LEARNING GOALS:

1. Identify the fundamental human values that define the relationship between customers and their ISP/cable provider.
2. Identify the ideal experience consumers seek along with an assessment of each competitor and Google Fiber against the ideal.
3. Develop a holistic brand platform that exploits competitive vulnerabilities and leverages brand assets.
4. Identify the precise feelings and emotions that motivate behavioral change.

HOMEWORK:

5. Please bring in 5–6 images that capture, communicate, or reflect the essence of the brand today.
6. Please bring in 5–6 images that capture, communicate, or reflect how your perception of the internet is today.
7. Please bring in 5–6 images that capture, communicate, or reflect your wishes for what the internet could be in the future.

PRE-SESSION:

Respondents are verbally rescreened by members of LLI team for articulation, enthusiasm, etc.

Moderator: Thanks for coming! My name is _____. I work for an independent research firm, so I'm not associated with any brands we'll be discussing today. During this discussion, there are no right or wrong answers and I want to hear from everyone. We are audio taping this discussion and behind the mirror. Some people are listening, and they may pass me a message during our discussion today. I'll also be taking some notes.

Moderator: Let's begin with introductions – each respondent introduces themselves:

Name, age, household composition? Occupation (current or former)? What do you use the internet for?

I. HOMEWORK DISCUSSION (30 min)

Moderator: Next, I want to confirm that all of you have brought your completed homework – please raise hands to confirm. OK! Please take out your HW images … we'll start with Question 1.

Q1. Brand Essence

Q1: Please bring in 5–6 images that capture, communicate, or reflect the essence of the brand today.

Place your 5–6 images from Q1 on table in front of you. Next, please select the most compelling image that best expresses your perception of Google's brand essence today.

Moderator Asks: Each respondent explains their top image and how it makes them feel, PROBES:

> Why does this image best express your perception of the brand essence?
> What does brand essence mean to you? Why?
> What is the main idea? Why is this image "best"?
> What feelings or emotions does this image evoke?
> What's the story behind this image?
> What does this picture tell me about what's most important to you?

Moderator probes homework images as a group:

> What is the story your other images tell?
> Do they relate to each other?
> What is the full story?

Moderator pins top images to wall.

> As a group, do they have anything in common? What ideals do these
>   images suggest?
> What feelings or emotions do they evoke?

Q2. *The Internet Today*

Q2: Please bring in 5–6 images that capture, communicate, or reflect how your perception of the internet is today.

Place your 5–6 images from Q2 on the table in front of you. Next, please select the most compelling image that best expresses your perception of the internet today.

Moderator Asks: Each respondent explains their top image and how it makes them feel, PROBES:

> Why does this image best express your perception of the internet?
> What is the main idea? Why is this image "best"?
> What feelings or emotions does this image evoke?
> What's the story behind this image?
> What does this picture tell me about what's most important to you?

Moderator probes homework images as a group:

> What is the story your other images tell?
> Do they relate to each other?
> What is the full story?

Moderator pins top images to the wall.

> As a group, do they have anything in common? What ideals do these images suggest?
> What feelings or emotions do they evoke?

Q3. *The Future of the Internet*

Q3: Please bring in 5–6 images that capture, communicate, or reflect your wishes for what the internet could be in the future.

Place your 5–6 images from Q3 on the table in front of you. Next, please select the most compelling image that best expresses your wishes for what the internet could be in the future.

Moderator Asks: Each respondent explains their top image and how it makes them feel, PROBES:

Why does this image best express your wishes for what the internet could
   be in the future?
What is the main idea? Why is this image "best"?
What feelings or emotions does this image evoke?
What's the story behind this image?
What does this picture tell me about what's most important to you?

Moderator probes homework images as a group:

What is the story your other images tell?
Do they relate to each other?
What is the full story?

Moderator pins top images to the wall.

As a group, do they have anything in common? What ideals do these
   images suggest?
What feelings or emotions do they evoke?

DISCUSSION ASSIGNMENT (1–2 min)

Moderator: Great job – now let me give you your official assignment – for
the balance of this you are my expert committee and your role is to help
me develop the best words and images to create the internet provider of the
future that will be most useful to you.

II. EMOTIONAL BENEFITS – FORM A (15 min)

Moderator: Prior to session's start, you were asked to review two forms
(A & B). Did everyone have a chance to review/complete this? Did you
underline key words/crossing out words you disliked? – Indicate your top
choices? Great – let's start with Form A first.
   Moderator: Next, we'll tally FORM A votes. If you voted for the statement,
raise your hand.
   Moderator: Probe rationale for top 3–4 statements:

What is the main idea of this statement? Why is it important to you?
What are the key words/phrases in the statement?

What words did you delete?
What feelings or emotions do you associate with this statement?
How does this make you feel?
Can you bring this story to life with an example from your life that illustrates this statement?

Moderator – pins top rated (1st or 2nd & 3rd choice A statements to wall)

Are any of these statements similar?
Are they identical?
If two statements are identical: Tell me why these are identical?
(If satisfactory): Let's re-order so the best expression is at the top. Which statement best expresses the main idea? Explain rationale.
If there is a tie for statement groupings: Can someone "make the case" for why this statement is best?

Moderator – Labels respondent built clusters with cards labeled: "A," "B," and "C."

III. VISUAL EXPLORATORY (25–30 min)

Moderator: Great job! (Initial sort) You've used words to tell me more about the feelings and values that are important to you – next I want you to look at pictures.

As you look at these images one by one, raise your hand /say "yes" if the image says something very positive and motivating to you about your life, your feelings and beliefs. If the image is not compelling to you, don't raise your hand.

As directed by respondents, moderator sorts images into 2 smaller piles – face up for "YES, COMPELLING" and face down for "NO, NOT COMPELLING."

Moderator: Re-sort Next, I want you to work together to sort all your "like/yes" images into smaller, homogenous groups and place the most compelling image on top of each pile, and give each group a nickname.

Moderator: Individual top images discussion:

How does this image make you feel?
What is most compelling about it?
What is positive and motivating in the image?

Moderator: Discussion of top-rated images pinned on wall (5 min)

Cluster Sort

Respondents link each top rated image to the A, B, or C clusters. If an image does not fit with any of the clusters, respondents can create a new cluster (D). PROBE:

■ Does this picture fit with any of our statements? Why/why not? Where does it fit best?
■ Explain rationale for placement? Repeat for all top rated images
■ When all images are placed into clusters – moderator asks respondents to agree on a thematic nick-name for each cluster. PROBE:
   What's the main idea of this Group A (then repeat for B & C) picture/ statement combo? Together, what story do they tell?
   What does the picture add to the words?
   Is there anything we could to do make this picture better?

Moderator: Thank you for giving me this insight into your values. Now I'd like to discuss what the ideal internet company must offer to be valuable to you.

Moderator hands out Form B.

I'd like you to now complete Form B – check top 3 selections, underline key words, and cross out words you don't like.

Moderator: Please raise your hand if you voted for the following statements.

Moderator PROBES: For Each Top Rated B Statement
   What is the main idea of the statement? Express in your own words.
   Key words? Why is this important? Motivating to you?
   Why did you pick it?
   Why is it important to an internet provider?
   Any suggestions to improve the wording – make it even more differentiated?

Moderator PROBES: Great job – Next I need your help to integrate your top-rated B statements into the clusters you're building:
   Guided by respondents, moderator integrates TOP RATED B statements into clusters, reminding respondents that they can create new clusters as needed. PROBE:

■ Do any of these ideas fit with our clusters? Why or why not? What are the linkages?

Moderator PROBES: Once B statements are integrated ... Moderator asks:

Has the main idea of this cluster changed? Are the nick names accurate –
do you still like them? (Repeat for each cluster)
Looking at the words and images together, what story does this cluster
tell?
What makes this cluster motivating?
How does it make you feel?
What does each cluster say about your ideal internet provider?
Is it unique/different from what companies there are today? Why?

IV. CLUSTER SUMMARY EXERCISE (15–20 MIN)

Respondents privately vote for their top-rated cluster and discuss rationale
for top choice:

Probe highest-rated cluster:

How does this cluster make you feel?
Does this cluster tell a compelling story or not about your ideal internet
provider?
What does this cluster say about you? About your wants from your internet provider?

Probe lowest-rated choice:

How does it make you feel?
Does this cluster tell a compelling story or not about your ideal internet
provider?
What does this cluster say about you? About your wants from your internet provider?

V. VERBAL SUMMARY EXERCISE (15–20 MIN)

Moderator Requests Summary From Respondents:

Next I'm going to pair you all up – Based on your top rated cluster, I want you to tell a friend a story as to why this internet provider is the best and most compelling choice – as if they're telling a friend "Dear Friend …", respondents use their own words to express the pitch that they believe would motivate men to select this company vs. the competition.

Respondents read their summaries and agree on the best story.

Moderator probes:

Would you buy this internet provider now? Why or why not?

Thank you and goodbye!

FORM A

DIRECTIONS:

Rank the options and SELECT up to 3 favorites

RANK your favorite 3 values/beliefs: 1=1st Choice, 2=2nd Choice, 3=3rd Choice

For each of your top choices, UNDERLINE words you like – CROSS OUT words you do not like.

Feelings and beliefs that are important to me:

1. Feeling connected to the people who give my life meaning.
2. Successful – at my best, personally, socially, and professionally.
3. Living life well – feeling healthy, happy, and fulfilled.
4. Confidence – knowing I can accomplish anything I set my mind to.
5. Caring for myself and the ones I love.
6. Being authentic – staying true to myself and others.
7. Living life to the fullest – making the most out of every day.
8. Being proactive – taking steps to change my life for the better.
9. Self-defined – living life by my own rules.
10. Being open to new ideas and experiences.

FORM B

DIRECTIONS:

Read all the options and SELECT up to 3 of your top favorite benefit statements

RANK your favorite 3 benefits: 1=1st Choice, 2=2nd Choice, 3=3rd Choice

For each of your top choices, UNDERLINE words you like - CROSS OUT words you do not like.

I would use this internet provider over other competitors if it...

1. Offers a seamless experience with easy-to-use products that integrate easily with my life and my home so I can focus on the important things
2. Gives me products designed for my and my family's needs and wants
3. Provides a tailored and personal customer service experience that puts my time and responsibilities first by anticipating my issues and following up
4. Provides the most up-to-date technology designed to answer the challenges of the ever-changing world around me
5. Is proactive about answering issues so my life isn't disrupted
6. Makes the process of subscribing to, installing, and using its services simple and easy to understand
7. Produces high quality products and services that require little to no maintenance and rarely experience issues
8. Integrates my user data to offer product and service suggestions for a personalized experience.

Index

Printed in the United States
by Baker & Taylor Publisher Services